Beating Depression Lifehacks:

52 way to overcome depression.

Alex Parker

ISBN: 9781976727863

www.beatingdepression.today

Dedication

To Taylor and Thomas. You kept me going and gave me the support and pushes I needed to carry on my writing.

Thank you

Contents

Acknowledgments

As always, thank you to everyone for encouraging me to continue writing. Since publishing my first book back in September 2017, it has been so great hearing from you all.

I am especially grateful to Jackie and Ian who got in contact via my website and have helped me improve some of my "Alex-isms".

We really are not alone and I dedicate this book to the Jackie's, Ian's, Thomas's and Taylor's of this world but also to you, the reader, who proactively look for ways to beat depression.

Introduction

A few months ago, I wrote a book on depression called *I'm Not OK, But I Want to Be* because I wanted everyone to understand how depression works and how it can be overcome. I've been open about my mental health struggles with my friends and family, and writing about it has helped me process my feelings and the difficulties I face. I'll probably struggle with depression to one degree or another for the rest of my life, and while I've found a good combination of medication and therapy to deal with particularly trying times, over the years I've also discovered things that help me cope when my mind and emotions feel overloaded.

I know they're not the ultimate answer to depression and I don't pretend that they are, but they do help me feel happier and better.

That's what we all want anyway, right? We want to feel better so that we can live our lives better as well. Here's the thing— aside from talking to a professional and working out the most effective therapy plan for you, one of the best things that anyone who's fighting depression can do for himself or herself is to develop and practice what I call **Depression Lifehacks,** specific things you can do that can help you feel better on days or seasons when it's hard to get out of bed and live life.

Depression is hard—no one needs to tell you that. The nice thing to know is that you're not alone, and knowing that others are finding ways to cope with it is comforting in itself. It's great to have options as to what you can do to give your spirits a much-needed boost when the blues come your way. They're not cures but they're part of the cure because they make life a little bit more livable.

So I've compiled 52 lifehacks, things you may want to try the next time you're feeling down and your soul needs a break—or an extra little lift to get you going.

If you have found this book useful, I would be grateful if you would leave a positive review on Amazon. I have just updated my blog website www.beatingdepression.today so please do check it out too! Thank you and I hope you enjoy and get something out of this this book.
Alex.

Lifehack #1:

Have A Real Bath!

Let's start off with one of my favorites! Skip your usual quick shower and have a good, old-fashioned bath with extra treats. Don't rush through this. You may want to soak for at least an hour and listen to some music, or even read a book. The point is to get away from the hustle and bustle of life and just take time to relax. Dermatologists have learned that baths reduce the levels of the stress hormone cortisol in our bodies. Less cortisol also reduces acne and delays premature aging.

Baths can also help lower our blood sugar level, and reduce our risk of diabetes. The nice thing about this lifehack is that you get to know your body all over again, especially the parts that you tend to miss out on like the curve of your hip or the back of your knee.

Here's a plus: baths are also better than showers for your skin, as you can add ingredients such as chamomile, rose, or tea tree oil to your bathwater to help moisturize or soothe your skin. If you have a bad sunburn or your skin feels particularly dry or irritated, you can add oatmeal to the water. Other, less well-known options for moisturizing your skin are honey and full-fat milk or heavy cream. Make sure to lather on some lotion as soon as you leave your bath as well.

Baths are also better than showers for relieving sore and aching muscles, as the heat in the water helps muscles relax. For a soak that's even more beneficial for your muscles, add Epsom salts. Just make sure the temperature of your bath water isn't too hot, as this could dry out your skin. Experts say that the perfect temperature for bathwater is toasty 112 degrees.

Pro tip: if it's warmth and heat that you're after, how about taking this to the next level by visiting a spa or a sports center with steam room and sauna?

This gives you a perfect reason to get up and about, since leaving the house for a while can definitely lift your mood. For more ideas on getting out of the house, there are a lot of other activities in this book that you can try.

Lifehack #2:

Light
A
Candle

There's something profoundly spiritual about lighting a candle, which is probably why people have done this in churches for centuries. Breathe deeply, light a candle, and stay still for a few minutes. If there's an area of your life where you feel some darkness, think about it and picture the candle lighting up that dark area. Candles have long been used for meditation and prayer as a powerful symbol of light and life. So you can use candles as you meditate, but make sure not to let your thoughts become too heavy. As you put out the flame, let go of the matters that are burdening you or causing you concern.

Candles, especially in the evening during cooler seasons, give off a warm, comforting glow. Nothing beats a candle for setting an intimate and cozy atmosphere. And when candles are infused with fragrant essential oils that help you relax, the effect is even more calming. If you like scented candles, make sure to choose scents such as lavender, vanilla, rose, or jasmine—these scents are proven to be calming and to aid in relaxation.

Some people enjoy lighting candles because they carry good memories of family holidays and festivities. If you want to combine lighting candles with soaking in a warm bath, you can turn off the lights and bathe by candlelight instead. Try it—it's a wonderfully soothing experience. If you're an early riser and it's still dark when you get up, why not light a candle instead of reaching for the light switch when you get up? This way, the light that surrounds you is gentle and soothing, easing you into your busy day.

Here is an affirmation you can speak when lighting a candle, if you prefer this to keeping still. From the wonderful Marianne Williamson.

"Our deepest fear is not that we are inadequate. Our deepest fear is that we are powerful beyond measure. It is our light, not our darkness that most frightens us. We ask ourselves, who am I to be brilliant, gorgeous, talented, and fabulous? Actually, who are you not to be? You are a child of God. Your playing small does not serve the world. There is nothing enlightened about shrinking so that other people won't feel insecure around you. We are all meant to shine, as children do. We were born to make manifest the glory of God that is within us. It's not just in some of us; it's in everyone. And as we let our own light shine, we unconsciously give other people permission to do the same. As we are liberated from our own fear, our presence automatically liberates others."

Lifehack #3:

Get Moving

There is a well-researched connection between depression and exercise. In fact, experts have called exercise the most under-utilized antidepressant known on this planet!

Take a walk or a bike ride or even a short run or swim—physical activity releases hormones into our bodies called endorphins, which are also known as happy hormones as they increase our sense of wellbeing. And, at the very least, exercising takes your mind off your stressors or the things that trigger depression. You may not feel like moving, but make a choice to get up and go and watch your mood lift as a result.

I have done some research and have found out that the six best exercises to beat depression are: yoga (so good that it deserves its own entry later in this book), dancing (ditto), hiking or trekking (more on getting out in nature later), lifting weights or strength training, running, and Tai Chi. Now, I've tried them all and found them to be equally effective, although personally, I find that running and strength training work best for me. However, I think it's great to have so many choices, since one of these is sure to suit your particular fitness regimen.

Since I'll be discussing yoga, dancing, and outdoor walks in depth later on, let me talk about the last three kinds of exercises—weights, running, and Tai Chi.

Researchers have shown that regularly lifting weights can help with both depression and anxiety by providing a boost to one's self esteem and mood. Lifting weights also causes reduced stress levels and leads to better sleep, both of which help with overall wellbeing.

All this to say—get moving. Try a simple workout, and see how the rush of endorphins gives your mood a boost.

Here's a quick, fifteen-minute workout with weights to get you started. It has only four exercises, which are:
• Dumbell goblet squat
• Bent-over row
• Deadlift
• Dumbell overhead press

Instructions: Do eight reps of the first two exercises without stopping. Rest for 30 seconds. Then do eight reps of the next two exercises without stopping. Rest again for 30 seconds. Repeat for fifteen minutes.

Or, if you'd prefer a CrossFit workout to weights, here's something you can do at home or at the park:

- 10 lunges
- 10 push-ups
- 10 squats
- 10 sit-ups
- 10 jumping jacks

Repeat 4 to 5 times, and voila! Instant home CrossFit workout.

As for *running*, well, there's a reason why there's such a thing as "runner's high," as running is very effective in releasing endorphins. Additionally, there's actually a study that shows that running is as good as talk therapy in helping to relieve depression.

If you have never gone running in your life, why not give it a try with this beginner's workout that will get you running for half an hour straight in just seven weeks?

- Week 1—run for 2 minutes, walk for 2 minutes (do this thrice in a week)
- Week 2—run for 3 minutes, walk for 2 minutes (do this thrice in a week)
- Week 3—run for 4 minutes, walk for 2 minutes (do this

twice in a week)

- Week 4—run for 8 minutes, walk for 3 minutes (do this twice in a week)
- Week 5—run for 10 minutes, walk for 3 minutes (do this twice in a week)
- Week 6—run for 15 minutes, walk for 3 minutes (do this twice in a week)
- Week 7—run for 30 minutes straight

Remember to walk for 5 minutes before every run to warm up, and then walk for another 5 after the workout to cool down.

As for Tai Chi, it's a deeply relaxing exercise that combines meditative movement with Chinese martial arts. People who regularly practice Tai Chi become less depressed or anxious and are able to handle stress better. A typical Tai Chi session enhances the mind-body connection, as practitioners concentrate on movement, balance, and relaxing both their breathing and muscles—all of which help stabilize one's mood.

Here is a quick, 15-minute Tai Chi tutorial of the top 10 Tai Chi moves for beginners.
https://www.youtube.com/watch?v=Yq3guYPRYzA

Lifehack #4:

Say Thank You

Say "thank you" to someone, because gratitude is a seriously effective mind hack. It could be to a friend or someone in your family. It could be to an old teacher. It could be to God or to the Universe at large. It's entirely up to you. There's a certain magic to the words "thank you" because gratitude and happiness are inextricably linked. People who are thankful are some of the happiest people around.

Let me give you an example. At the coffee shop I frequent, I now thank the barista every time they make my hot chocolate with extra whipped cream. They smile, and I smile. This little exchange is a boost of sunshine to my day, and I now enjoy getting my daily cup!

The feelings of gratefulness add to overall feelings of happiness and therefore reduce depression. How does this happen? There are three reasons:

1. When we're thankful, we dwell on the positive instead of the negative events on our lives, which leads to

2. A surge of happiness-inducing hormones such as oxytocin, dopamine, and serotonin, and

3. We also end up strengthening personal relationships and connections when we express our gratitude, and relationships are key to lasting happiness. So we can easily see how gratitude is a win-win-win.

Here are some suggestions for saying "thank you."

- Write down 3 things that make you happy for 21 days and track how your mood changes.
- Write a letter to someone you haven't seen in a long while but who had a profound positive effect on your early years, such as a teacher or babysitter.
- List the acts of kindness you received today.
- List the acts of kindness you performed today. You'll end up grateful that you had the strength and resources to make them happen.
- Write down the funny things that happened in your life in the past month.
- Write down the negative things that happened in the past that actually turned out for your good, though you had no way of knowing it at that time.

Then, do a little self-examination after you did any of these exercises. How do you feel? Chances are, being thankful and expressing your thanks has made you a whole lot happier. This is something that's good to remember.

One more thing you can do is to have a thankfulness board or journal. Put the letters and lists into the board or journal and display it where you can easily see it in your room. This way, when things are rough, you can easily take the journal out, or look at the board, and have visual reminders of the good things in your life.

Lifehack #5:

Get Some Sun!

Surprise, surprise—but the amount of sun you're getting can affect your mood. The number of people who get depressed spikes during months when there's more darkness and less daylight, from the months of November through March, at least.

Plus, there are a lot of holidays during these months that trigger certain expectations with loved ones—Thanksgiving, Christmas, New Year's Day, Valentine's Day—and when these expectations go unmet, as they do for so many of us every year, the fact that they occur during cold, dark days can be a double sadness whammy.

Doctors have discovered that how much or how little sunlight and darkness a person is exposed to determines the release of certain hormones in their brain. The more sunlight you get, the more your brain releases the hormone serotonin, which is a mood-booster and helps you stay focused and even calm. Conversely, exposure to darkness causes the release of the hormone melatonin, which makes people sleepy.

So the more sunlight you get, the more serotonin your brain produces. The less sunlight, the more at risk you are for SAD, the apt acronym for Seasonal Affective Disorder, which is one kind of depression brought about by a change in seasons.

Go out during your lunch break and look up, feel the sun on your skin. Make it a point to spend weekends outside in nature, or take a day trip to an outdoor activity such as a farm or an amusement park. If this is not possible and you've got a case of the winter blues, there are effective lamps and light boxes that mimic the beneficial effects of sunlight specifically made for people affected with SAD.

The release of serotonin occurs through the sunlight that passes through your eye. Sunlight triggers a cue in the retina of your eye, which then causes the release of serotonin. Bundle up on sunny days even when the weather is cold, just to get out and get your brain to produce serotonin.

What more can I say? The sun can definitely make us feel sunnier and there is nothing better than waking up and seeing the sun rise or seeing it set after a busy day.

Lifehack #6:

Words Have Power

No, I take that back. Words *are* power. Words carry the power to bring light or darkness to you. We've all experienced this, right? We've received compliments or kind words that brought a lift to our spirits, and conversely, we've been on the receiving end of insults or nastiness that led us into dark moods. So a mantra can bring brightness to your day. Try something like, "This too shall pass" or "I am a child of the Universe."

Mantras are essentially repeated sounds or words that get past your conscious mind and vibrate throughout your whole being. You can use a mantra by saying it repeatedly out loud, practicing it in your mind, or by simply listening to it recited. It can be a single word or a phrase or a sentence that is repeated to attain a specific goal.

A mantra can be a powerful tool to take you into a better state of mind and mood, since they are words that are full of intention and energy that promote positivity, healing, and growth or relaxation and calmness, depending on what you need at the time. Each person can have a tailor-made mantra for their particular situation.

Mantras can be repeated as many times as you like. It is also a good idea to set aside twenty to thirty minutes each day to say or listen to your mantras.

Interestingly enough, many people who say their mantras discipline themselves to do so consistently for forty days at a time to ensure the most positive and beneficial results. I'll be giving examples of some wonderful mantras in the bonus section at the end of this book!

Lifehack #7:

Color

There's been a recent trend in the publication of coloring books for adults in the past few years, right? The creative act of making something beautiful, even if it's mainly beautiful in your eyes, isn't only relaxing, but it can also be powerfully life-affirming. You'll even be pleasantly surprised to find some talent that you never thought you had when you were younger.

The famous psychologist Carl Jung used coloring many years ago to help his patients connect with their subconscious. There are also a number of psychologists today who use coloring as a substitute to meditation, to help patients calm down and relax. When coloring, people concentrate on putting color to complex illustrations, and are therefore diverted from their own busy thoughts. Coloring can also aid people in shifting their focus away from their negative habits and problems and direct them to a productive and creative endeavor. Activities like coloring causes our amygdala to calm down—the brain's center that keeps us in fight or flight mode and causes us to be overly vigilant. Simply put, coloring helps our brain relax and rest.

Coloring is also beneficial in that it brings us back to a happier time in our childhood, when we had less responsibilities and did something for the sheer fun of it. It therefore helps remove you from whatever stressful situation you have at present, even for a temporary respite. At the same time, coloring is good for your brain because it actually helps you concentrate and focus. I'm being perfectly serious here, coloring activates our frontal lobes, where concentration can be found. You can think of coloring as therapy, which is designed to lessen how anxious and stressed we feel, because it is. And in the process, you end up with a piece of art that you can frame or stick on your refrigerator door—two benefits for the price of one, so to speak.

Lifehack #8:

Go on A Gadget Break

I've always felt that social media is a mixed bag of blessings and...well... otherwise. On the one hand, it's great to get connected and caught up with friends whom you haven't seen in years. on the other hand, it can also be a real cause for envy and even discouragement, like when you see the seemingly perfect lives that other people have and compare them with your own. Plus, the 24-hour news cycle of what really is a lot of bad news in the world today certainly doesn't help when you have anxiety or depression. Take a break. Switch off for a little while. You'll find that when you get back on, you'll be better equipped to handle what you see and hear.

A few nights a week, I switch my phone off from 10pm until 6am and actually put it in the far recesses of my wardrobe so that I don't get tempted to check my social media accounts if I wake up in the middle of the night.

You've probably heard fitness experts say that sitting is the new smoking, right? A sedentary lifestyle is apparently even more dangerous today than lighting up. But it's possible that it's not merely sitting itself that's causing us harm, but the many hours of brainless scrolling that we do on our social media accounts that is also responsible for some of the damage.

The jury is still out on whether internet addiction is a real thing, but more and more people believe that it might be, since it manifests some of the same patterns of other addictions, such as escapism, neglecting one's social life, experiences that can cause mood swings, etc. And people who suddenly quit social media after participating heavily on it also experience a type of withdrawal.

So, why not take a break? Give yourself a breather if you've been using Facebook, Instagram, and Twitter too much. Go outside and go for a walk, or spend some time with a friend or loved one. You'll be pleasantly surprised at the emotional balance you'll regain.

Lifehack #9:

Read

A

Book

When was the last time you picked up a book and read it from cover to cover? Obviously, well done for reading *this* book! If you're anything like me, you may have picked up half a dozen books over the last few months—and put them down again without finishing them. Sound familiar? But one way to feel better is to pick up a book you can commit to from start to finish. Bibliotherapy is a real thing.

There are practicing bibliotherapists who ask you a number of questions about your life and then come up with a list of recommend books for you to read. As a result, more and more people are discovering the therapeutic effect that books can have on our minds and moods.

But even if you never visit a bibliotherapist, here's a good place to start. Read books that can inspire you, like travel or transformation journeys, or literary fiction that allows us to escape into the different worlds of various people you don't know, in times and places you've only dreamt of but come to care about and emotionally invest in as you read about their lives.

Or, read a fast-paced bestseller—a thriller or "beach read" romance or family saga—it's entirely up to you. Choose what you like best. Similar to meditation, reading brings our brains into a happy state that is trance-like, and also gives the same benefits to our health such as inner peace and deep relaxation.

People who read regularly experience better sleep, decreased levels of stress, as well as higher self-esteem than non-regular readers. As Shakespeare wrote, "Come, and take choice of all my library/And so beguile thy sorrow..."

Here are some recommendations for an uplifting read:

- **The Little Prince** by Antoine de Saint-Exupery
- **Sophie's World** by Jostein Gaarder
- **To Kill a Mockingbird** by Harper Lee
- **And the Mountains Echoed** by Khaled Hosseini
- **Gift from the Sea** by Anne Morrow Lindbergh
- **The Lives of a Cell** by Lewis Thomas

Lifehack #10:

Put on Your Best Clothes

It is really important that we are self-aware of how we project to others. Make sure you've paid attention to your grooming and that you walk tall with a smile on your face. It's an old adage, I know, but there's more than a grain of truth to it—*when you look better, you feel better.* You get a psychological boost when you look your best.

For me, I enjoy wearing a pair of polished brown leather shoes with fitted jeans, a white shirt, and a blazer. I know it sounds a little casual, but I feel great when I'm wearing that outfit. How about you? What outfits do you own and enjoy wearing? Conversely, what outfits do you not enjoy wearing and why do you still wear them?

Dr. Samantha Boardman says this, "Next time you are having a bad day, skip the sweats and throw on your favorite outfit, something you know you look and feel great in." I couldn't agree with her more! When you were a little kid and played dress-up, how did you feel when you changed into that superhero or princess or dinosaur costume? More importantly, how did you act? Putting on something new made you change the way you behaved, right? Putting on a costume, which is just a new set of clothing, can made us feel braver, smarter, more capable, more attractive, etc., right?

So what is your favorite outfit? Why do you like it? Does it give you more confidence? Do you feel better when you wear that outfit? If so, think about what you like about the outfit and see whether you can replicate that feeling with other outfits.

Clothes can have magical powers that way. Now, everyone has outfits, dresses, separate tops and pants, accessories, and shoes that look great on them and have perhaps gained them compliments in the past, or just given them extra confidence when they've put them on. Or we have clothes that have good memories attached—we were wearing this shirt when that special thing happened, and wearing it again makes us smile. Try this sometime.

On a day when you feel extra tired, moody, down, or cranky, wear something that makes you look and feel terrific. Fix your hair well and, for the women, pay attention to your make-up to finish off the complete look. It's a small thing that can go a very long way.

Though remember, if you don't feel good regardless of what you wear then I think you need to be considering the underlying reasons for why you are feeling the way you do. The purpose of this book covers tips to jump start your journey to beating depression and will skip out the identifying, analyzing, understanding side of depression as I talk about this in a lot more detail in my first book. I am a strong advocate for becoming aware of oneself and identifying why you feel the way you feel and then identify how best to move forward.

Though to return to clothes – If you feel it is just that you don't like your current clothes – start saving or head for a thrift store and shop for that new look!

Lifehack #11:

Take A Nap

Yes, yes, I know this isn't rocket science but really—a nap has amazing restorative powers. I'm talking about a power nap of twenty minutes, maybe thirty minutes maximum, not sleeping for so long that you won't get a good night's sleep tonight. When you're feeling particularly drained or listless, a nap can reset your day.

Naps have been shown to uplift your mood and improve your memory, help you re-focus, as well as help you feel better all around. Researchers have also found out that naps help your brain work better. It's called a power nap for exactly that reason! But make sure to keep it down to just thirty minutes, as anything longer than that can leave you disoriented or irritable, or even interrupt your nighttime sleep schedule, which is very important for your emotional, mental, and physical health. But if you are tired, lay your head down somewhere and go for a catnap, power nap, micro-nap, or whatever you choose to call it. Your mind and body will thank you later on.

The nice thing about naps becoming more and more popular is that you see more napping places or pods in airports, offices, and even malls. Additionally, one nice thing to note is that some very famous people were proud of being nappers as well, such as Bill Clinton, Sylvester Stallone, Nikola Tesla, Eleanor

Roosevelt, Albert Einstein, Leonardo da Vinci, Winston Churchill, and John F. Kennedy. Go on. You know you need it. Take a nap knowing you're in good company.

So, the next time you feel blue and tired and you've got about twenty minutes to spare, lie down. Go on, try it. If there's nowhere to lie supine on your back, just lay your head down on your desk on top of your folded arms.

Extra tip: for instant relaxation, I plug my earphones into my phone and play a white noise app called White Noise. There are others, such as Chroma Dose and Sleep Fan, all of which are free on GooglePlay. I usually put on something that has the sound of water falling, like Rain on a Car Roof, but there are so many options to choose from. Don't forget to set your alarm so you can get up and go back to work!

I recently started listening to a song called Weightless by Marconi Union. It really chills me out and helps me drift off for a fantastic nap.

Lifehack #12:

Watch Some Cartoons

Okay, fine, it doesn't have to be cartoons, but choose something light and pleasurable for you—such as a romantic comedy or a favorite TV sitcom, that will get you laughing and help you experience a needed lift in your mood. For me personally, nothing beats Rick and Morty or a well picked Japanese anime, and there is something to be said about cartoons, so bear with me here.

First of all, the themes in cartoons can help you when you're feeling troubled. There's an emphasis on friendship, community, and family, the triumph of good over evil, and that tomorrow will be better than today. They are apt to leave you optimistic as well as provide you with a distraction from whatever you're feeling at the moment. Plus, watching an animated show can be beneficial in that it's sometimes easier to watch animated characters struggle with real-life issues and situations. Animator Tony Celano says, "Animation lightens the load of a normally rough subject. If a character in live action runs into a wall, we wince. If a cartoon does it, we laugh at the slapstick humor."

Cartoons help us because in watching them we apply what the medical field calls *opposite action*—participating in an activity that you don't necessarily feel like doing but it diverts you from your feelings of anxiety, stress, anger, or sadness—in order to stabilize or modify your emotions. So, one of the things to do when you feel down is to make yourself laugh with cartoons. People have called laughter "the best medicine" for years, and I will not underestimate its therapeutic effects, which extend to the point of laughter being recommended by the Mayo Clinic as one way to relieve stress and tension and boost your immune system.

What is your favorite cartoon? I personally have got into Rick and Morty at the moment – I cant explain why other than to say it has the right degree of dark humor and slapstick humor that I enjoy!

Lifehack #13:

Stop and Smell the Essential Oils

Essential oils are proven to be effective in uplifting our moods. As our brain processes smells, it sets off emotional responses in your limbic system. Smell is the sense that is closest to memory and even certain emotions. I have a history of insomnia and had first heard about lavender's calming effects years ago. To be honest, I wasn't expecting much when I first tried lavender oil in a diffuser, but that night I slept like a baby. That convinced me that essential oils are pretty powerful. When you're feeling blue, here are some scents that can help lift your mood.

- *Bergamot oil* improves the circulation of blood in the body and causes you to feel fresh, joyful, and energized. It has also been proven to reduce anxiety. Rub a few drops of bergamot oil in your hands and gently breathe in, cupping your hands over your mouth. You can also rub bergamot oil on your stomach or feet.

- *Lavender oil* has been used to fight depression, anxiety, and insomnia for years. If you have a diffuser, diffuse lavender oils near your bed at bedtime or wherever you choose to wind down and relax. Alternatively, you can also rub lavender oil behind your ears.

- *Chamomile oil* encourages relaxation and combats stress, which is one of the reasons that chamomile teas and tinctures have become quite popular. Like bergamot, chamomile oil can also be inhaled.

- Inhaling **Ylang ylang oil** does not only fight off depression but other negative feelings that come with it, such as envy, low self-esteem, and irritation or anger. Ylang ylang also has a gently sedating effect that helps people feel more relaxed and calm.

If you don't have an oil diffuser, here's a DIY hack. Soak a cotton ball in your favorite essential oil and put it on a saucer, or mix some drops of your favorite essential oil with water and spray it into air in the room where you relax or even where you work. You can even spray some of the mixture on your bed to create a relaxing space for you to sleep.

Lifehack #14:

Project Paint

Proponents of the psychology of color are convinced that the colors you're surrounded with affect your wellbeing. It's isn't purely an aesthetic matter, but is about which shades can be used to promote your emotional, physical, and mental health. Let me give you a quick rundown of which hues are best for the different rooms in your home.

- Your bedroom may be the most important part of the house, as it is where you relax and get rested and replenished. It's best to choose cool colors here—think lavender, green, or blue, as they contribute to feelings of calm. The color blue slows down your heart rate and lowers your blood pressure. The first thing I did when I moved to my apartment was to accent my bedroom with shades of blue to make it as relaxing as possible, because getting a good night's sleep is vital to my health—and to yours, too.

- The living room and dining room may work best with earth tones (beige and brown) or warm colors (orange, red, and yellow). These hues encourage conversation and connection.

- For the kitchen, if you had a happy childhood, experts say that you may want to paint your kitchen in the same colors as the ones from your childhood home. Or, warm colors such as the reds, oranges, and yellows used in the living room are also a good choice. PS—if you're watching your weight, you may want to stay away from the color red, which is known to stimulate one's appetite. Ever notice how many fast food joints are red? Enough said.

- Bathrooms are traditionally white, but if you want to relax in your bathroom and turn it into a mini-spa, then choose the same relaxing blues, purples, and greens.
- If you have a home office—green may be the best color for you, as it promotes concentration and productivity.

Lifehack #15:

Watch Your Favorite Funny Movie

Remember what I said earlier about cartoons and opposite action? It may sound a little simplistic, but this really works. Psychologists have learned that things that make you laugh out loud—or even smile, for starters—can trick your brain into believing that you're actually happy. Bring out copies of your favorite rom-com, no matter if you've seen it many times before. If you don't want to watch anything and reading is more to your liking, bring out the book that never fails to make you laugh, or look up your favorite comic writers online. Their latest blogs will cheer you up. Laughing can decrease pain and stress hormone levels, plus boost your immune systems.

Let me give you some suggestions for great laugh-out-loud comedies.

- **The Full Monty**—come on. Six questionably attractive guys doing striptease for work. Loved it back in the '90s, and it still makes me laugh today.
- **National Lampoon's Vacation**—Chevy Chase taking his family out on vacation is hilarious. Several sequels followed this first movie, but IMHO, the original is always the best.

- **Monty Python's Meaning of Life**—this is sketch comedy at its finest. Several original members of the troupe are all together here, which makes it a real treat.

- The **Pink Panther** movies. Go old school with Peter Sellers, or the newer one with Steve Martin. Both versions are a hoot!

- Speaking of Steve Martin, he has an early movie called **The Jerk** which is a comedic classic. This one's a can't-miss.

- **Animal House** is equal parts raunch, good humor, and John Belushi. Guaranteed to make you laugh.

- **There's Something About Mary**—We all knew Cameron Diaz was gorgeous, but she is also unabashedly, unbelievably funny in this movie. And this is my favorite Ben Stiller movie...with...

- ...**Zoolander**—coming in a close second. Ben Stiller and Owen Wilson as dimwitted and gorgeous male models who end up fighting crime...or more importantly, Will Farrell.

- **Airplane!**—True confession time. When I'm really down in the dumps, *Airplane!* is my go-to movie. This film ranks in the top 5 of every "Funniest Movies" list I've ever seen, that's how good it is.

- **A Fish Called Wanda.** This may just be my favorite movie of all time. Seriously, you cannot find comedy better than what Kevin Kline, John Cleese, and Jamie Lee Curtis do in this movie. Outstanding!

Lifehack #16

Try Something New

This can be as simple as mixing up your morning routine or changing the route you usually take to school or work, or something more complex like signing up for a walking tour of your city (or the city that's nearest you.) There's most likely a restaurant or coffee shop that just opened near you that's worth a visit, or a museum in your town you've never seen. Maybe it's a new short-course class that will sharpen your skills or even create new ones. Doing new things opens the pathways for dopamine in your brain, the hormone that is in charge of rewards.

Trying something new also causes you to cross an invisible boundary—fear of the unknown. This is a good thing because it makes you more courageous. There are only two possible outcomes to this—you'll either like it or you won't. The important thing is that you tried it out, because if you never try, you'll never know.

Trying new things actually gives you the opportunity to discover new things to enjoy. They also offer relief from the routine of everyday life and give you something to look forward to. See new things as exciting challenges and opportunities for growth.

Here are a few possible new things you could try:

—learning a new language

—a country's cuisine you've always been interested in but have never tried before

—a sport or other physical activity such as a hot or hanging yoga

—a musical instrument (it's never too late to try the cello or the clarinet)

—start drawing, maybe start with an adult coloring book and then work out what you like to do and go from there!

Lifehack #17

Spend Time In Nature

There is nothing like being out in Mother Nature to lift one's mood. It could be as simple as taking a walk in the park to something as complex as joining a wilderness therapy program, depending on your interests and fitness levels. Being outdoors increases mindfulness, calmness, and relaxation. Additionally, being outside usually involves some form of exercise or another. Exercise increases endorphins, as is well known, and exercising outside also increases self-esteem as well as decreases tension, anger, and sadness.

Researchers have also found out that the greatest advantages of exercising outdoors occur within the first five minutes, which means you don't have to spend a whole lot of time on it.

As long as you can manage it and the weather permits it, how about trying to spend at least a few minutes every day or every other day outdoors? We've already seen the benefits of serotonin releasing sunlight, making going outdoors a doubly beneficial activity. In hot weather, try to spend a few minutes outdoors early in the morning or before the suns sets, and in cold weather, come out when the temperature is highest. And your activities need not be strictly exercise either—you can fly a kite, go sailing, or even sit outside and eat lunch on the grass.

Here's a possible lifehack—how about aiming to walk at least a kilometer a day, and build it up from there. Doctors recommend that we walk at least 10,000 steps per day, which is about eight kilometers. But for starters, since the average pace of a person is five kilometers per hour, walking one kilometer should only take you twenty minutes. It's a good place to start!

Brad M. Reedy, PHD, who directs clinical services for Second Nature Wilderness Programs, says, "Gratitude and mindfulness, beauty and serenity are inherent in nature. The silence of nature quiets the mind and offers a person the opportunity to get in touch with the core of the self."

I am considering taking a month trip (need to keep saving though) and travel through south east Asia as I really want ot spend some time out of the country but also in nature. I can also tick off my "get some sun" lifehack and I am sure a number of others in this book all at the same time!

Where would you like to travel and go? It doesn't have to be a big trip – where can you go and still be close to home? How do you feel about getting to know nature a little better?

Lifehack #18

Volunteer

Now, you might think volunteering is counterintuitive when you feel out of sorts. You might feel some self-doubt because you're having a hard time taking care of yourself as it is, and your brain may seem a little muddled, so why should you even think of volunteering to care for others? Don't worry about it. Volunteering doesn't just benefit the organization that you help, but is of great benefit to volunteers as well.

For one thing, volunteering causes you to forget about your own situation. For whatever amount of time you spend volunteering, you get to focus on the job instead of your feelings. Secondly, volunteering boosts feelings of pleasure. It simply feels good to do good. Helping others brings great happiness. Third, volunteering also helps you grow in self-esteem and confidence, because you realize that the work you're doing has great value to those you're helping. Finally, spending time with other people widens your circle of friends and acquaintances, which is really good for your social life.

How do you know what organization to volunteer for? Well, why don't you start with your personal interests. If you like small children and are good at interacting with them, then volunteering to spend time caring for them, playing with them, teaching them art, or telling stories to them is a good idea. If you miss your grandparents and feel a special connection with the elderly, then volunteering at a seniors' residence is right up your alley. If you love the environment, check out the local groups who are doing beach cleanups or tree planting activities. If you do not love animals, then for goodness' sakes don't apply to volunteer at an animal shelter, right?

Here's another big plus when it comes to volunteering: one of the best things about volunteering for an organization whose advocacy is close to your heart is that you get to make friends with people who share your passions. What's good for your social life is good for your emotions, too.

Lifehack #19

Create a DIY Feel Better Kit

This is a small bag that you'll open up on days when the megrims hit you. It's like an emergency or first aid kit for your mind and emotions. How do you do this? Set aside a bag—a backpack, tote, drawstring bag, etc., and put some survival items in it that will help you on dark days.

What kind of items, you might ask. Well, here are some suggestions:

- *Your favorite chocolate bar.* No, I'm not telling you to "eat your feelings." But sometimes, just a few bites of something we love and associate with positive emotions can calm us down nicely.
- *A weighted blanket or a favorite pillow.* Weighted blankets are great for making you feel safe and secure— honestly, they can be a good substitute for a hug when you're by yourself. And your favorite pillow automatically gives you extra comfort.
- *Notes to yourself.* A few encouraging lines such as "Everything's gonna be all right," "The sun will come out tomorrow," or "This too shall pass."
- *Hand lotion in your favorite scent.* Mine is The Body Shop's Mango Body Butter, or anything vanilla or coconut scented. Smelling things that you like makes you feel better.

- *Herbal Tea.* A sachet or two of peppermint, ginger, chamomile—or any fruit tea combination. You don't want to get the caffeinated kind, lest it add to your stress. Choose a relaxing flavor that will help you unwind.

- *A beloved book or audio book.* So you can curl up somewhere with an old favorite, and wile away the time pleasurably.

- *A heating pad or cooling ice pack.* Heat soothes sore muscles that have been tensed up because of anxiety, and cool packs help you calm down when you're feeling particularly anxious.

Photos of people you love. When I'm feeling blue I like to look at old photos of my mom and dad when they first got married, me and my siblings when we were small, and even photos of my best friends in high school. I miss all these people, but looking at their pictures never fails to make me smile.

Lifehack #20

Forgive Someone From Your Past

Maybe it was someone who caused you a lot of pain or said hurtful things to you that you find hard to get over. Maybe it was someone who doesn't understand depression and put you under pressure to just "choose to be happy." Maybe it's an old girlfriend or boyfriend who left you and broke your heart. Forgive them. It's one of the hardest things to do. Let go of the hurt or hard feelings you had concerning them, like a child lets go of a balloon and watches it fly away. You may have to say to yourself, "I forgive XXX," more than once. In fact, you may have to say it several times like a mantra, but after a while you will feel a weight off of your shoulders when you forgive.

Studies show that forgiveness leads to greater happiness, and this positively affects one's mental health. Conversely, unforgiveness—that is, holding on to a grudge against someone, can negatively affect one's health. Self-forgiveness has long been part of therapy sessions and is key to one's personal growth, but interestingly enough, forgiving others is proving to be even more beneficial. A study conducted in 2014 found that those who forgave the people who wronged them tended more to let go of negative feelings, which gave them a chance to concentrate on the positive aspects of their lives.

However, it's possible that you've suffered terribly because of abusive people in your past and you may not feel ready to forgive them yet. That's all right. Forgiveness should never be forced. You can begin to say to yourself that you will be ready to forgive them one day and let go of the pain that they have caused you.

Now, if you are ready to forgive those who did you wrong, here are some ways to do it.

- **Make a conscious choice to let go of your anger and/or hurt feelings.** It won't feel great right away, but we all know that our feelings follow our choices, so making this choice is the first step.
- **Vent your feelings—once and for all.** Put it all out there, whether in a letter, your journal, or a phone call or conversation with someone. Find someone you trust and tell them exactly how you felt when your wrongdoer did what they did to you. Get all your pent-up feelings out, so you can get them out of the way.
- **Refuse to think of yourself as a victim any longer.** Because you're not. Your past is in the past and you put it actively behind you. Make a choice that you are not allowing what your wrongdoer did to you to have power over you anymore.
- **Think of how far you've come today.** Focus on all the good you have at present—that you're still here, alive

and kicking, with people who love you and a purpose to fulfil on this earth.

- **Make another conscious choice—this time to stop reliving and remembering the past.** Time to fill your mind with thoughts of the future, and how bright your tomorrows are.

- **Forgive yourself, if you need to.** Sometimes we're very good at blaming ourselves for our past mistakes, and we actually find it easier to forgive others than to forgive ourselves. In fact, depression makes it easy to rehearse how much we've messed up in the past. Take a deep breath and let go of even your own shortcomings. Perfection is the enemy of humanity, and everyone messes up, even you.

Lifehack #21

Occupy The Mind With Games

This is really good for getting your mind off of yourself and focused on something else, even for just a short while. It's good for your brain not only to be diverted from your current mood, but to actually concentrate on solving something. The satisfaction you'll feel afterward will be well worth it.

Puzzles can help decrease your levels of stress and anxiety and lift your mood. Matching puzzle games like *Candy Crush* or *Bejeweled* are helpful because they make the outward distractions in your life seem smaller, thus making you feel less stressed.

So where do you start? Well, flea markets and garage sales are a good place to find inexpensive boxed puzzle sets, some of which have never been opened. Choose something with a few hundred pieces in a design you like, and set it out on an unused table in your house. You may want to get it all done in one go, or you can leave it open and work on it a little bit at a time, whenever your mind needs a break. Famous producer Michael Codron calls it "making order out of chaos," and that's a good exercise for your mind when you're feeling stressed or anxious. It will help calm you down.

Personally, I prefer digital puzzles on my phone. After a long day in front of my laptop when I don't want to do any brain work anymore, I go back and forth between *Candy Crush, Fishdom, Gardenscapes,* and *Gummy Drop.* Not the most sophisticated choices, I know, but hey, to each his own, right? These are all free games, and more importantly, they cause my mind to relax and help me to transition between the day's work and getting some rest at night.

More excellent mobile puzzle games are:
- Monument Valley
- Threes!
- Framed
- Blek
- Scribblenauts Remix
- Trainyard

There's something for everyone. Simply download them, and you are good to go.

Lifehack #22

Attend A Yoga Class

(or practice Yoga at home)

Yoga can be a huge depression and anxiety buster. Since breathing is a big part of yoga, when you breathe deeply, your stress response system gets relaxed, and you end up feeling calmer and more centered after a good yoga session. The nice thing about yoga is that you master the poses the more you do them, so when you need to practice a relaxation technique on your own, you don't even need to wait for the next class to begin. Yoga causes you to be more attuned to your body, which is a good relaxation technique as well.

All aerobic exercise releases endorphins and raise the levels of dopamine in our brains, which makes us feel better. But some types of exercise are even better than others, and yoga has been proven to have especially beneficial therapeutic advantages for people who experience depression. Some people swear by "hot" or *Bikram* yoga, which involves different positions and breathing exercises designed to heal our bodies' different systems, while others prefer *Hatha* yoga, where you combine *asanas* (positions), controlled breathing, and brief moments of deep relaxation.

Yoga also helps with blood circulation in the body by increasing the delivery of oxygen to our bodies' systems. As I mentioned earlier, yoga also helps us regulate our breathing to make it stable and calm, sending relaxing messages to our brain. It also regulates our bodies' stress response systems and encourages mindfulness, which has proven to be helpful with depression and anxiety. One more benefit of yoga is that it also gives you a community of fellow yogis who are often nurturing and who can provide a support system for you.

Here are five poses you can do to calm yourself and to ward off depression:

1. **Child's Pose—**Kneel down, and sit back on your heels. Bend forward until your chest is on your thighs and your forehead is resting on the floor. Drop your shoulders forward and with your palms up, let your hands rest on the floor at your sides. They should be right by your heels. Hold this pose for five to eight breaths.

   Benefit: This is a resting pose that reduces stress and eases your mind.

2. **Bridge Pose—**Lie down on your back with your knees bent and your feet flat on the floor, hip distance apart. Place your hands along your body, palms side down, with your fingertips grazing your heels. Inhale and lift your hips, rolling your spine off the floor, planting your feet solidly on the ground. Keep your knees at hip distance. Lift your buttocks up, engaging your legs, and pressing your shoulders unto the floor. Hold for 5 to 8 breaths, then release gently, rolling

your spine back onto the floor.

Benefit: This exercise provides a gentle stretch to your back and legs. It reduces insomnia, anxiety, fatigue, headaches, and backaches. It can also help lower your blood pressure.

3. Standing Forward Bend—From a standing position, exhale while bringing your arms down and your palms flat on the floor, bending your knees slightly and resting your forehead on your knees. Feel your spine stretch. Straighten your legs to feel the stretch even more. Hold for 5 to 8 breaths, and then relax your arms to the sides, and then gently raise your arms and torso back to a standing position.

Benefit: This exercise stretches your hamstrings, thighs, and hips. It also relieves stress, depression, and fatigue.

4. Cat Pose—Get on your hands and knees and exhale, drawing your belly to your spine and causing your back to arch. Make sure to round your back upwards. Draw the crown of your head toward the floor, gently moving your chin to your chest. **Benefit:** This pose relieves stress and stretches and soothes your lower back while massaging your spine.

5. Corpse Pose—Lie flat on your back with your arms at your sides and your palms toward the ceiling. Make sure your legs are relaxed and not touching. Keeping your eyes closed, take deep breaths. Pay attention to each part of your body, starting with your head and moving down. Stay in this position for 5 to 7 minutes.

Benefit: This pose is for total relaxation and puts your body completely at ease. It slows down your breathing, lowers your blood pressure, and calms your nervous system.

Lifehack #23

Start
A
Journal

Another successful depression buster is journaling, which is simply writing your own life down. Journaling has two main aims—one, to recapture certain specific moments in the day and how you felt and what you thought during those moments; and two, learning from those moments when you've examined them, since writing about them usually gives you keen insights about you and the world around you.

Writing is effective in combating the blues because it's a great tool for self-knowledge. The more you know about yourself— your triggers for sadness or anger, what causes you joy, etc.— the better you'll be at overcoming depression. When you need to track the points when your self-talk or self-reflection are no longer healthy, keeping a daily journal is extremely helpful in pinpointing those thoughts and examining their origin, so that you can make necessary changes.

Helpful tips on starting a journal:

- Aim to write daily. This is more successful in developing a habit rather than telling yourself you will write on the occasions when you feel like it. Set aside the same time every day for journaling, let's say before you go to bed, or before you leave for work or school in the morning, and devote at least 20 minutes of your day just for writing.

- Make sure you are undistracted when you write—this will ensure that your words flow freely. This means putting your phone on silent for a while, and telling your partner, roommate and/or kids that you need some uninterrupted time.

- Not sure about where to start? Here are some things you can jot down. Don't self-edit, your grammar, mechanics and punctuation don't need to be perfect. Be your rawest, most honest self as you talk about how you **think** and **feel**, the **ideas** that came to you that day, the **issues** that concern you, what you got done as an **accomplishment** that day, what **disappointed** you, your **interactions** with others.

Write it all out—the good, the bad, the beautiful, the ugly. Writing can be a wonderful, stress-relieving, creative act.

Lifehack #24

Sing like You're In the Shower!

Singing as a hack for depression? Yes, indeed, because when we sing, we release endorphins, similar to what happens when we exercise. Happy hormones flood our brain and change our mood for the better. It's been well known throughout the ages that "Music has Charms to soothe a savage Breast," as William Congreve famously wrote. Yes, depression can feel like a savage has taken up residence in your chest, and on certain days when you find it hard to even breathe, music, especially singing, is there to calm you down.

Another hormone that gets released when we sing is oxytocin, the hormone responsible for feelings of connectedness and intimacy. Additionally, people who sing regularly have lower levels of cortisol, a stress hormone, in their bodies. Singing by yourself is an effective mood booster, and singing with others has even more benefits.

So what can you do? If you would like to sing with others, here are some suggestions:

> • *Join a choir or a capella group.* Yes, you can. A good place to start is your local church, of course. Many churches today don't require you to be a member in order to join the choir—although clergymen and women are always hoping you'll love being in the choir so much

that you'll end up joining the church anyway. But there is a heartening and surprising rise in non-religious indie choirs and a cappella groups in many parts of the world, and some especially cater to a certain demographic (LGBT etc) and some where you don't have to audition at all.

• *Set up a karaoke night with friends.* These can be unbelievably fun as well. Ask some close friends to join you at a karaoke joint on a Friday or Saturday night and get ready to let loose your inner Jay-Z or Beyonce or Mariah Carey. You don't have to be great at singing to feel great—in fact, the more you can laugh at yourself, the better you will feel. Will you be incredibly nervous at the start? You better believe it. Just do it—as Nike says—tummy butterflies and all.

But what if you're the shy type and want to try singing on your own first? That's cool, too. You can:

• **Play your favorite song and sing along.** Sing to your heart's content. If you haven't memorized the lyrics, that's what our old friend Google is for.
• If you want to do karaoke at home and don't have the machine, **YouTube** has amazing **karaoke channels** such

as Sing King Karaoke, TheKARAOKEChannel, Karaoke on Vevo, etc.

Singing is an excellent depression hack! Not only does it make you feel happier, it also builds your confidence, is empowering, and when you sing with a group, you build good connections with other people. Think of the a cappella groups in the "Pitch Perfect" movies that are so close, they're almost like family.

Lifehack #25

Dance Like No one's Watching

This list would not be complete without mentioning dancing as an amazing depression life hack. As I have said so many times in this book already, any form of exercise is beneficial when you are fighting the blues, but there is something about dancing that brings about a special kind of joy. Put on your favorite music and start dancing away, and even if you don't feel like it, I can almost guarantee you that when the song is done, you'll be in a much better mood. Maybe the reason why dancing is such a powerful depression booster is that it's a happy marriage of two amazing things that individually make us happy—music and movement.

Dancing has proven to be helpful in boosting both self-image and self-esteem. It helps build better communication skills and memory. It lifts your mood and promotes optimism, as well as curbs aggression. There is a strong connection between mood and movement—people who are very sad barely move at all, while people who are agitated can't stop moving. Since dance is an art form that is self-expressive, people's movements when they dance help them communicate what and how they feel.

Let me share some of my happy dance music with you: "Walkin' on Sunshine," by Katrina and the Waves, "R-E-S-P-E-C-T" by Aretha Franklin, "The Love Shack" and "Roam" by the B-52's, and of course, Pharell's "Happy."

But how? And where do I start? How about—

- Find a class nearby. Different folks like different dance styles. **Zumba** is very popular these days, and is one way to get your groove on. Or there's also **Hip-hop**—if that's more your jam. If you loved **ballet** as a child, and found that it always centered you, then look for an adult ballet class nearby. Or if you've never tried it before and you always wanted to—how about an adult beginner's ballet class? If modern **jazz** is something that gets your blood flowing—look for a local jazz class. Some people really enjoy **tap** dancing, and why not? You just might find the rhythm of the steel tips on the floor to be oddly comforting.

- You can also try ballroom dancing. This is great fun if you like dancing with a partner, and learning the different styles can certainly be uplifting. There's the **mambo, Cha Cha, rumba, foxtrot, Vietnamese waltz, paso doble, jive, quickstep, tango, lindy hop, samba,** and don't forget the regular **waltz.** Why not challenge yourself and see how many you can learn in six months or a year?

- So you feel self-conscious and want to try dancing at home by yourself. No problem. YouTube has so many fantastic dance tutorials that are easy to follow, again, depending on what dance style you prefer. If you have no idea where to start, here are some possibilities. These are all less than 7 minutes long, and so much fun to do.

- Option 4 is the simplest. All you need is your favorite dance song. Plug in your earphones, or blast your favorite song on full volume on your speakers, and let your body go where the music takes you!

Have at it. The wonderful thing about dancing is that you don't need any special equipment or clothing to do it. You don't need a barre, a mirrored room, or an audience. Just let the music lift your feet, and I guarantee you your spirits will follow!

Lifehack #26

Get (and give) Some Good Hugs

Hugging, snuggling, and cuddling are surprisingly good for us. Studies show that getting close to and being held by someone releases oxytocin to your brain and helps combat anxiety and depression. There is even new research that shows that babies who receive enough cuddling may possibly never develop depression later on in adolescence and adulthood.

Giving and getting hugs also strengthens our connections with other people, something that's very important, since depression can sometimes isolate us from our loved ones. It may not feel easy to give and get hugs, especially if you've been isolated for a while, but when you are with people who care about you, those whom you trust and feel safe with, why not try something along the lines of:

"Hey, I'm really glad to see you. Mind if I give you a hug?"
"Have I told you how thankful I am for you? Can I give you a hug?"
"I miss you, and I want to tell you how much you mean to me. I just want to give you a hug right now."
"I don't think I've hugged you enough recently. I really appreciate you."

You'd be surprised to feel how wonderful a good, old-fashioned hug is, especially if you stay in that position for more than a few seconds.

What if I have no friends and family nearby? I understand that some of us live far away from our loved ones or don't see them on a regular basis. In this case, many therapists recommend getting a dog or a cat, who are wonderful sources of affection and devotion. If this is not possible, find someone you know who has a dog or cat and offer to help take care of their pet. You can take your friend's dog on walks, or bring their cat to the vet for grooming and spend some time playing with or cuddling it.

Physical touch really can have amazing restorative powers. A wise man said that children need four hugs a day for maintenance and eight for growth. I think this should hold true for adults as well.

Lifehack #27

Do *Something* Creative

Creativity is power. Creativity has to do with thinking up with new ideas, making new connections between ideas, as well as discovering new solutions to old problems. And here's some exciting news: scientists have discovered that creative people are some of the happiest people on earth!

But what if you've never been artistic in your life? Not a problem. Anyone can be creative, though we all have different ways of expressing it. The main thing is to be open-minded. You don't have to be stuck in thinking of traditional artistic modes. You can apply your creativity to cooking, budgeting, or even entrepreneurship—by thinking up new business ideas, for example.

Whatever means you find to express your creative side, it's good to know that there's a strong link between general happiness and expressing yourself creatively. In fact, getting into a creative "flow"—that state of being so deeply immersed in what you're creating that you become unmindful of any other distraction—can bring about sufficient happiness that outlasts even the joy you get from eating a delicious dessert. Which is really cool, because everyone knows how happy desserts can make us, right?

Now, I do understand that when you're in a depressive funk, the last thing you might feel like doing is to be creative. I get how you feel. But I do suggest that you push yourself a little bit to participate in a creative activity—whether it's writing a poem, drawing something, cooking a dish like a boss, working on a business model—whatever floats your boat. When you find yourself in that creative zone, I guarantee that you'll feel so much better.

There are some things you can try to help your creative juices going

- *Lego (or any other kind of building block) set—* There are so many lego sets to choose from, it's almost crazy. They range from sets of blocks for basic creativity to building your own town. If you're a Star Wars fan you can build the Millennium Falcon, and Disney fans can build Elsa's castle from Frozen. Science geeks can make their own Lego robot with sensors, motors, and software, while history buffs can have their own version of the US Capitol Building. The sky's the limit when it comes to Lego sets.

- *Try out a new recipe.* Here, if you've never baked bread, is a basic recipe that is just delicious and doesn't need any fancy equipment either.

Ingredients

1 pkg yeast (active dry, 1/4 oz)

2 and 1/4 cups warm water (45 degrees)

3 tablespoons sugar

1 tablespoon salt

2 tablespoons oil (canola)

6 and 1/2 cups flour (all purpose)

Instructions

Dissolve yeast in warm water in a large bowl. Add 3 cups of the flour, along with the sugar, salt and oil. Beat until the mixture is smooth. Add the rest of the flour one half cup at a time, until a soft dough is formed. Put the dough on a surface sprinkled with flour, and knead for around 9 minutes until the dough is smooth, with an elastic surface. Put dough into a greased bowl, and turn over and grease the top of the dough. Cover with a towel and allow dough to rise for about 1 hour and fifteen minutes, until it doubles in size. Punch the dough down, and place it back onto a floured surface, cutting dough in half. Place each half into a greased 9 x 5-inch loaf pans. Cover again and allow dough to rise to double its size, for around 40 minutes. Bake dough at 190 degrees for 30 minutes, until you see the tops are golden brown. Pro tip: Tap the surface of the bread. When it sounds hollow, it's done. Cool on wire racks and enjoy!

- *How about a fashion design kit?* A company called Seedling has a "New York Fashion Design Kit" complete with a tiny mannequin, fabrics, a sketchbook, pencil, and pattern shapes. In other words, all that's necessary to design and sew tiny clothes. You can choose between the kit with red and blue fabric or one that comes with greens and blues.

- *How about creative writing?* You can try Louie Stowell's Usborne **Creative Writing Book.** It comes with all sorts of writing prompts, tips, and exercises for writing poetry, stories, screenplays, comic bold, and teaches how to write outlines, interesting characters, and dialogue. It doesn't matter if you prefer to write adventures, romance, or scary stories, this book has it all, even tips for wanna-be journalists. Yes, I know it's for kids, but I also think that we're all just big kids at heart.

- *Create a mini-animation studio.* You can get the StikBot Animation Studio from Toy Shed. It comes with two tiny people with suction cups in their hands and feet, and a special app for Android or iPhone with a green screen function that gives you all kinds of backgrounds, or allows you to create your own, for your very own animation movies.

- ***Become a face painter.*** Or at least have fun painting your own or other people's faces. Snazaroo's Ultimate Party Pack Face Painting Kit comes with twelve colors, brushes, sponges, and glitter gels so you can transform into all sorts of fantastic creatures. Fun to do on your own, and take lots of pictures, or invite a few friends to come over and paint each other's faces—and take even more photos.

Lifehack #28

Put Your Legs Up

Now, I can hear you thinking, 'Are you kidding me?' Hang on! Before you slam this book shut—or close the tab and switch on something else on your e-reader—let me tell you something. Lying down with your legs up and resting against the wall is probably one of the simplest and quickest ways to get into a state of deep rest. This position is not only good for your nervous system, but it's also great for your heart, legs, internal organs, and your circulation. Don't even think of reaching for your next caffeine jolt and going on with the rest of your day when you can take 5 to 10 minutes in this relaxing pose.

This is a restorative yoga position, and the only equipment you need are a floor and a wall. It's actually my favorite yoga position—I love it even more than the child's pose. Within 5 minutes in this position, you will feel relaxed and energized at the same time.

Okay, so how do you get into this pose? You may want to have a cushion or a rolled-up towel on hand before starting. With your left side leaning against a wall, sit down with knees bent. From this position, turn and bring your buttocks near the wall, while leaning on your elbows. Make sure that your lower ribs, stomach, and pelvis are all aligned. Move your legs up the wall gently, making sure to stay relaxed (no need to rush). If the muscles in the back of your legs feel tight, or if you feel that your backside is lifting up, stay at a little bit of a distance from the wall (no need to achieve a 90-degree angle). The important thing is that you feel comfortable in this position because you want to relax, after all. If you need to, place a small cushion or rolled up towel under your head, so that your chin is lower than your forehead. And make sure your neck and shoulder muscles are comfortable and not tense. Put your arms at your sides with palms facing upward. Practice breathing deeply and feel your legs relax.

When you're ready to get up, don't do so suddenly. Drop your knees to your chest gently, and then roll onto your right side. And give yourself a little bit more time before getting up, enjoy the feeling of being relaxed and calm. (For the ladies—if you're pregnant and past your first trimester, or if you have your period, this is not a recommended pose for you for the time being.)

Lifehack #29

Bask In Good News

Yes, I know that much of the news that comes out nowadays is bleak, and in fact, we are constantly bombarded by a 24-hour news cycle of tragedy and suffering. This is terrible, especially when you're already struggling with feelings of melancholy or worry.

But here's the thing. There is actually a lot of good news in the world—acts of kindness and goodness that don't make the headlines since they don't have the same kind of impact that negative news does. But there are many kindhearted people in the world who are doing wonderful things with Mother Earth, animals, and our fellow human beings. Reading about them can give you a major uplift to your soul and inspire you to contribute to the good in this world. In this way, reading about good news is also empowering, because you end up thinking, *if this person can change the world, so can I.*

My favourite happy news site used to be The Happy Newspaper (https://thehappynewspaper.com) a wonderfully upbeat online news site with stories of incredible goodness in the world. The author has since taken time off her site to write a book, but her Instagram account is still active @thehappynewspaper, and the print newspaper is still going strong. But aside from The Happy Newspaper, there are many other online sites that provide inspiring and uplifting news such as

- https://www.sunnyskyz.com/good-news
- https://www.positive.news
- https://www.goodnewsnetwork.org

Even your favorite news site such as the BBC, The Mirror, The Telegraph, Today, and Huffington Post have their good news sections, and all you have to do is turn to these pages.

http://www.bbc.com/news/av/world-39461779/the-week-s-happy-news

https://www.today.com/news/good-news

http://www.mirror.co.uk/all-about/feel-good-news

https://www.huffingtonpost.com/topic/good-news

http://www.telegraph.co.uk/good-news/

Unconvinced? I think some sample headlines from these sights will put a smile on your face:

Girl With Down Syndrome Graduates High School... With Honors

https://www.sunnyskyz.com/good-news/2489/Girl-With-Down-Syndrome-Graduates-High-School-With-Honors

Three good things: harnessing human energy for good

https://www.positive.news/2017/science/30100/three-good-things-harnessing-human-energy-for-good/

Shelter Dogs to Get Temporary Homes So They Can Celebrate Thanksgiving With Families

https://www.goodnewsnetwork.org/shelter-dogs-get-temporary-homes-can-celebrate-thanksgiving-families/

4-year-old girl donates piggy bank money to police officer with cancer

https://www.today.com/news/girl-donates-piggy-bank-money-police-officer-cancer-t118140

Quick-thinking train guard "saves" two young women from "creep" they hadn't spotted watching them

http://www.mirror.co.uk/news/real-life-stories/quick-thinking-train-guard-saves-11116604

Pets And People Are Joyously Reuniting After California Wildfires

https://www.huffingtonpost.com/entry/california-wildfires-pets-animals-reunions_us_59ed0ffee4b0a484d063f434?utm_hp_ref=good-news

Brixton riding school brings joy to inner city kids

http://www.telegraph.co.uk/good-news/seven-seas/brixton-riding-school/

Lifehack #30

Do A Random Act Of Kindness

In the same way manner as volunteering, being kind can do wonders for your mood. Especially when your kindness is truly random, and done for no reason, or to someone or some people you don't know. Kindness builds empathy in us and helps us walk in someone else's shoes for just a little bit and understand their situation. Kindness and empathy help us build stronger relationships with each other.

Someone once said, "Be kind, for everyone you meet is fighting a hard battle." Studies have shown that people who have done good to others experience a greater amount of happiness than those who only do good things for themselves. This is because acts of kindness raise serotonin levels, the hormones that contribute to well-being and satisfaction.

Furthermore, being kind to others also boosts endorphins and causes what psychologists call "helper's high" wherein people feel more accomplishment and connectedness. This sets in motion even more feelings of happiness. It's a good kind of chain reaction.

Here are some suggestions for acts of kindness:
- Give a stranger an honest compliment.
- Hold the door open for someone.

- Send an email to someone you haven't heard from in a long while.
- Flash someone a big smile.
- Offer to help out an elderly friend or neighbor.
- Bring pastries, muffins, or doughnuts to work.
- Pay for someone behind you at a tollbooth or drive through.
- Bring your favorite dish to a sick friend or a mum who just gave birth.

Take a week and do an act of kindness for someone every day. It helps you and others at the same time.

Lifehack #31

Organize *Something* In Your House

When you feel out of sorts, tackling a part of your house that needs to be cleaned out can help lift your mood. Think of all the clutter in your home accumulating in various storage spaces. Think of all the paper that's stacked up over the last years, such as bills, letters, cards, restaurant takeout menus, flyers, catalogs from grocery stores, etc. Think of the seasonal decorations, old photos, and mementos that are lying around, begging to be organized. Cleaning the house, or even part of your belongings, can help you feel better and more in control.

One organizing trick you can adopt is the ABC method.

A—Assess the situation. If it's papers you're organizing, go ahead and gather every piece you have all over the house, from your mailbox to various counter or table tops, to bedside drawers and fridge doors.

B—Box or Bin? The next step is to determine what you'll keep (box) and what you'll throw away (bin). Pro tip: If you haven't used something in a year, it's probably time to toss it out or set it aside for donating to charity.

C—Control. Sort out all the papers you have, and put them in different piles for bills, letters, government notices, etc.

Also, here are some easy organizing tricks that you can try

- Use a shoe organizer, the clear plastic kind that you can hang anywhere. In cold weather, put one on the back of your front door for scarves, hats, and gloves. Hang one up on the garage wall for nails, tacks, and other small items; put one in the bathroom for toiletry supplies, another in the kitchen for spices and small sachets of mixes. How about one in your linen cabinet for small towels and pillowcases? These hanging organizers make things so orderly.

- Put all the instruction manuals for your appliances and gadgets into an accordion case, complete with their receipts, warranty cards, etc. This way, they're all in one area whenever anyone in the family needs to access them.

- Tired of plastic bags everywhere? Place them into an empty tissue box, or if you prefer something more fancy, a nice tissue holder.

- For organizing your closet—how about dividing your clothes into several categories such as work, casual, formal and sportswear? Take it one step further and put all the skirts or slacks together, or organize them according to color. It makes dressing up a whole lot easier.

- How about hanging up the pots and pans in your kitchen,

especially if they look nice and can serve a decorative function?

- Keep a "Drop Zone" basket on your kitchen table—a repository for things you need often like keys, sunglasses, charging cords, wallets, etc.

You can also implement your own organizing system with your books, music, and photos and files on your laptop, phone, or computer, but there's an extra advantage to actually getting up and moving around. Putting things in proper order can also give you a strong sense of satisfaction and accomplishment.

Lifehack #32

Stand Up Straight

Our physical posture, more often than not, reflects how we feel. When we are confident and sure of ourselves, we stand up straight and hold our heads up high. In the same way, when we're sad and upset, we tend to stoop and slouch, and it's hard for us to hold our heads up, let alone look people in the eye.

The good thing is that we can trick ourselves into feeling better simply by changing our posture.

Try it the next time the blues hit you. Sit up straighter, and see how your mood changes. Researchers are beginning to trace the connection between mood and posture, and have learned that sitting in an upright position increases feelings of self-worth, endurance in problem-solving, as well as confidence. It also causes you to be more awake and energetic and feel less afraid, even after activities that are difficult.

Would you like to give it a try? Here's a step-by-step guide for improving your posture:

When standing
—your weight should be mostly on the balls of your feet
—your knees should be slightly bent
—your feet should be kept shoulder-distance apart
—hang your arms down naturally to the side

—picture a string at the crown of your head pulling up, and let your shoulders follow, letting them be pulled backwards

—keep your stomach tucked in

When sitting

—keep your feet on the floor

—keep your legs uncrossed, with your ankles in front of your knees

—keep your knees below your hips

—keep your shoulders relaxed and pulled back and your arms parallel to the floor

This works in the same way that putting on your most attractive outfits and grooming yourself well on days you feel "off." Your mood follows what you put on, and your mood also follows how you position your body. It's a little like tricking your mind and emotions to feel better when you're down, but these mind tricks work for your good.

Lifehack #33

Take Deep Breaths

We've already seen how regulating your breathing during yoga can help you relax and feel less stressed, but on the days when you don't have the time and space to do yoga poses, taking deep breaths all the way from your belly can have the same beneficial effect. Deep breathing increases our bodies' oxygen supply and helps relax and calm us down.

Let me show you two exercises for deep breathing.

First, close your eyes and give your full attention to your breathing. Place one hand on your chest and another on your belly. Time your breathing so that your chest and belly rise and fall at the same time. If they don't, it means your breathing is still shallow. When you are breathing deeply, your body will relax, and your mind will seek positive, rather than negative thoughts.

Put your phone on silent and take an interrupted break for this exercise, preferably in a place where you are alone. The fewer breaths you take per minute, the deeper your breaths are.

For the next exercise, sit on a chair, keeping your feet flat on the floor and your back straight. Raise both arms, inhale, and hold your breath. While your breath is held, make fists and squeeze them, letting your muscles tense up. Exhale, and as you do, put your arms down slowly and with resistance, as though you were pulling on something. Repeat 5 times.

On the final breath, cross your arms over your chest and drop your chin down. Inhale 4 quick breaths in succession without exhaling and hold your breath, then exhale through your mouth. Repeat the 4 quick breaths several times, focusing on your breathing.

Lifehack #34

Spend time with four legged friends

Stroking a cat's fur and hearing them purr is deeply calming and relaxing, and if you are a dog person, playing with some frisky pups is a surefire way to chase the blues. You'll find your energy level rising up to match that of the little guys you're playing with.

I actually read an article whilst I was writing this book about a study that took place in Sweden that showed that owning a puppy/dog could actually help you live longer!

The study was investigating the effects of <u>cardiovascular diseases</u> and after looking at over 3.4 million people from Sweden (<u>Swedes</u>) who were between the ages of 40-80 – the results showed that spending time with your four legged friend could in fact help you live longer!

Pet owners have a much lower blood pressure than those who don't, and people in recovery from heart attacks heal more quickly with pets in the home.

What more can I say? These furry, four-legged friends are good for us. A good friend once told me, "When you want uncritical, unconditional love, get a dog." It's true! Dogs will love you to the moon and back, and when they do, it's for life. They won't offer their opinions, judgments, or trying-to-be helpful advice. They'll just look at you, love you, and try to get as close to you as they can. On the days when you're feeling extra fragile or vulnerable, cuddling with a pet can be invaluable.

And pets are lovely to come home to. You may have had a really trying day at work, but when your pet welcomes you when you get home, things are instantly a little bit better. They're good company too when you don't really feel like talking but you don't want to be alone either. They're also such a good distraction.

It's hard to be in a bad mood when the kittens or puppies around you are playing. Additionally, when pets demand to be stroked or touched, this can actually boost the amount of happy hormones like serotonin and dopamine in your brain.

Added tip: Don't tell my dog but I would love a cat...

Lifehack #35

Prepare And Eat A Really Healthy Meal

Processed foods, as satisfying as they are in the moment of devouring a whole bag of chips or a great big slice of chocolate cake, can unfortunately increase a person's chances of getting depressed. That can sound like a real bummer, but instead of thinking about that, try to concentrate on all the good things that good nutrition can do for your body, including the opposite effect of boosting your mood and making you happy.

Whatever makes your body more healthy is also good for your brain, such as sufficient rest and sleep, sunshine, fresh air, lots of water, and yes, good nutrition. The nutrients that contribute to good brain health are Omega 3 fatty acids (fish, seeds, nuts), Vitamin D (bread, milk, juices), Selenium (chicken, walnuts), B vitamins (meat, green leafies, seafood, eggs, whole grains), and Tryptophan (turkey, beef, dark greens). Sounds yummy, right?

So the next time the blues hit, why not plan a few meals around these superfoods for your brain? Find some recipes that incorporate these foods, and build a simple menu around them. Your mind, as well as your body, will thank you afterwards. To make these meals even more special, use your good china, your best linens, and decorate your table well. Why not even invite a friend over for your home-cooked meals, and make eating a social endeavor that brings you joy?

I have a whole chapter in my first book which gives you a number of recipes to try. For now, here are three more healthy recipes that will help your mind and body function well, and that taste simply delicious.

Healthy Pork Curry

Ingredients

1 tbsp. coconut oil

400 gas lean pork, diced

1 tsp turmeric

1 onion

2 cloves garlic

1 tbsp. ginger, grated

1 large red chili pepper, finely chopped with seeds

removed

1/4 c malt vinegar

1 and 1/2 cups boiling water

2 cups grated cauliflower

1 cup red, brown, black or Basmati rice

20 ml Greek yogurt

2 tsp garam masala powder

Instructions:

Mix pork with turmeric. In a pan, put oil, onion, garlic and ginger and cook over medium heat until vegetables are soft. Add pork and stir fry for 5 minutes. Add vinegar, chili pepper, garam masala and boiling water. Simmer for half an hour. Remove from heat and add yogurt. Mix well.

Cook rice. Just before rice is done, place grated cauliflower in a steamer above the rice. When rice is done, mix with cauliflower.

Serve the pork curry with the rice-cauliflower mix. Enjoy!

Walnut-Zucchini Bread

Ingredients:

450 gm grated zucchini	1/2 cup chopped walnuts
4 cups whole meal flour	1/2 tsp pepper
2 tsp yeast	2 tbsp. olive oil
1/2 cup grated Parmesan cheese	warm water
	milk

Instructions:

Drain the grated zucchini in a colander for thirty minutes. Dry with a paper towel afterwards. Mix the yeast, cheese, walnuts, and pepper with the flour. Add the oil and zucchini to this mixture. Mix very well, adding water to make a dough that's firm. Sprinkle flour on your counter and knead the dough until it's smooth. Put dough back into the bowl, cover with saran wrap and let rise in a warm place until the size of the dough has doubled. Take from bowl and lightly knead, and then put it in a greased loaf pan. Brush the top of the dough with a little milk, and let it rise again. Bake in a preheated oven at 200 degrees until golden.

Poached Figs in Red Wine

Ingredients:

18 fresh figs

600 ml Italian red wine

225 grams white sugar

Instructions:

In an aluminum saucepan large enough for all the figs, place the wine and sugar and cook over medium heat until sugar is dissolved, stirring with the wooden spoon. Lower the heat. Place figs gently into the pan, and simmer from 8 to 10 minutes, after which figs should be deep brown and very tender. Being careful not to burst the fruit, remove figs gently with a slotted spoon, placing them in a serving dish. Keep cooking syrup for another six minutes or so, until syrup reduces. Pour syrup on the figs and serve when cool.

Lifehack #36

Deliberately...

Slow Down

I kid you not, the pace of modern life is undeniably fast, and it feels like things get faster every year. Everyday life is so jam-packed with so many activities that every night we get home exhausted, only to start all over again in a few short hours, and we think this is just normal life. All we want to do when we get home is relax, but often, we carry our workload and problems into bed with us, causing our sleep quality to suffer because our minds don't get the rest they need.

Even while we're commuting home or during weekends and vacation time, we still get urgent texts and emails from our bosses and/or clients that need an answer ASAP.

And sometimes, you just have to say, "Enough of this. I am not going to let this hectic, multitasking life get the better of me!" To help you do this, put your phone on do not disturb mode and/or change your emails from push to you need to login, so that all these seemingly urgent tasks are not hounding you.

Slow things down. This can do wonders for your mental health. You're not much use to your partner, family, boss, or company if you're overloaded and frazzled, irritable and stressed. Slow things down—you need this.

But how? One practical thing is to get up 5 to 10 minutes before everyone else in your household does, or before you normally do, and sit down and start your day with some quiet time. Resist the urge to reach for your phone. During your lunch break, don't just gobble down your meal but eat slowly and deliberately, savoring every bite. Don't just rattle off texts and emails like an automaton but give yourself the time to read what you are responding to carefully, and craft a reply.

When working, do one thing at a time, and don't start a task until you're done with the first. Refuse to multitask, if multitasking only makes you more frazzled and less efficient. Train your brain to work at a slower pace—it can bring such sweet relief.

Lifehack #37

Practice Mindfulness Meditation

Meditation has been proven to help people who experience depression, anxiety, and even pain. Even devoting less than half an hour a day to meditation can bring about positive effects.

Mindfulness meditation teaches your mind to remain in the moment. In order for this to happen, in this practice you're taught to relinquish your hold on anxiety for the future as well as regrets from the past, in exercises such as the 'body scan' wherein you are guided into relaxing the muscles of every part of your body, starting from your jaw, down to your neck, your shoulders, and all the way down. This way, you check in with the different parts of your body to see if there's tension in any part.

Let me also give you an example of what's been an effective mindfulness visualization for me. I sometimes get bothered by thoughts that cling to my mind and won't seem to let go. I picture the sky in my mind and see the stubborn thought detaching from my mind and attaching itself to a cloud in the sky, and then I visualize the cloud floating off. This has helped me rid myself of some pesky, bothersome thoughts, and I'm left with clarity and calm.

Here are two meditation exercises that you can try.

1. In a room where you won't be disturbed or distracted, sit upright either on the floor or in a chair. Facing a blank wall would be ideal for this exercise.

2. Make sure you are seated comfortably enough to allow you to focus on your breath rather than any discomfort you may feel. If you're on the floor you might want to sit on a cushion, and if you're sitting on a chair, you may want to choose one with firm back support, rather than a couch or recliner. You want to sit up straight while you are meditating, as this makes breathing easier.

3. Face downwards, and put your hands flat on your lap. Keep your eyes open, and let your hips be higher than your knees.

4. Sit still for some minutes, concentrating on the present. Stay conscious of your body, your posture, and the surroundings. When your mind wanders, re-focus back onto the present moment.

5. After concentrating on the present for a while, turn your focus to your breathing. Concentrate on the air coming in and out of your lungs. Put your full focus on the natural rhythm of your breathing right now, and don't try to breathe in any special manner.

6. Along with your breathing, stay aware of your body and your

surroundings. Concentrate on both the present and the rhythm of your breath. When your mind wanders, always go back to the present.

7. After a few minutes of focusing on breathing and on the present, let your mind wander. Don't censor or evaluate your thoughts, just let them flow freely. Whether they are worries, memories, your to-do list, or scenes from movies you've watched, there is no need to control them. Just let them come to you. You might even provide a narration for your thoughts, such as, "That thought was from the movie I saw last night." Or "That's a financial concern I have right now," or "I remember that from when I was 10 years old."

8. When you've spent around 20 minutes to half an hour just letting your thoughts flow freely, and you find yourself in a relaxed and calm state, you can end this mindfulness meditation exercise.

The second exercise is called a lovingkindness meditation.

1. Sit in a comfortable position on the floor and begin a mantra. Out loud, say what you want in life, for example, "Today, may I be patient, calm and relaxed. May I do good to everyone I meet. May I receive blessings at work and at home." Go ahead and recite more things that you wish for.

2. Afterwards, in the same way, start speaking good wishes or blessings to people you know. "May my spouse/partner be

blessed with abundance." "May my child be filled with hope and love." Direct good thoughts and wishes to different people in your life who you are thankful for.

3. If there is someone in your life who you are ambivalent toward or even have difficulty with, send them thoughts and wishes of lovingkindness as well. When you send goodness to people who have wronged you, or who you find hard to love, you are actually empowering yourself.

4. To end this mediation, send lovingkindness to the whole world, saying something like, "Let everyone on the earth today be showered with joy and surrounded with peace."

Another option is to find a guided meditation technique online, or even order some guided meditation CDs or mp3 files. These meditations can have a wonderfully calming effect on you on days when you feel depressed or anxious.

Here's a guided mediation for positive energy.
https://www.youtube.com/watch?v=RZQ9GfmzR14

Here's another one with an uplifting affirmation to start your day.
https://www.youtube.com/watch?v=7lscI5-f420

Here's one more for healing—this one is a personal favorite of mine.

https://www.youtube.com/watch?v=rEXa_3ELy_o

Experts say that it's good to aim for two and a half hours of meditation weekly, as this has been shown to improve depression symptoms. One thing you can do to help yourself to meditate regularly is to incorporate it into your daily routines. For example, you can schedule in 20 minutes of meditation after you wash your face when you get out of bed in the mornings, or maybe at night, between brushing your teeth and going to bed.

Lifehack #38

Write A Letter

Because I love to write, this depression hack comes naturally to me, but as natural as it is, it doesn't mean it's easy. If you write a letter you might as well be painfully honest about how you really feel, otherwise what's the point? It is this honesty that brings relief and release from the painful feelings that depression brings.

Some suggestions for writing a letter when you feel depressed

- Write a letter to yourself as a child. Tell your 10-year-old self what life is like right now, what's good about it, along with what isn't going well. Tell little you all about the qualities you'll need as an adult to not just survive but to thrive in our world today—things like outspokenness, courage, grit, perseverance, a sense of humor, or levity. Tell him or her about your greatest achievements along with your biggest disappointments, your heartaches and your joys, your deep regrets and your hopes for the future.

- Write a letter to someone close to you. You have the option of sending this letter or keeping it, that's entirely up to you. It could be your best friend or any one of your close friends, your brother or sister, parents or grandparents (living or departed). But it should be someone you care deeply about. What should you tell them? Whatever's in your heart.

- Write a letter to depression. Tell it exactly how you feel about it and what it does to your mind, body, relationships, work, etc. Don't hold anything back. Don't be polite. If you're angry at depression for all the lies it has told you over the years, then write all that down. Don't stop until you've got some peace. Tell depression that in this fight, you are stronger and you will not let it win.

In your writing, be vulnerable, be honest, and be hopeful for the future. You have the final say. If you do write to someone else, make sure you keep a copy for yourself. This will help you track your progress later on. Place your letter in an envelope with the date written on it. Keep a file with the letters you've written. Plan to revisit your letters after three or six months or so and read them carefully, so you can see how far you've come. If there are action steps and goals that you said you would do, re-reading the letters will help you be reminded of them.

Lifehack #39

Do The Things You *Used* To Enjoy

Even when you don't feel like it...especially when you don't feel like it. Remember opposite action? This is pretty much it in practice. When you're depressed, it's really easy to stop showing up for the things you used to love to do—like Sunday afternoon baseball games, or Saturday morning trips to the organic market, or chess games with your dad, or bowling with your co-workers. Even little things like walking around town, going to your favorite coffee shop, or buying freshly baked bread from the bakery, can give you a degree of joy. Unfortunately, depression can sometimes make staying in bed and sleeping in look more attractive than any of these things.

Don't give in. Even if you have to psych yourself up to get ready for these activities, and then go through the motions for the first few minutes, that's all right. You don't have to experience the same enjoyment as you used to all at once. The fact that you're still at it, that you made a choice to show up, gives you a chance to rekindle the enjoyment you once had for these activities.

This is where Nike's famous swoosh and logo comes into play. "Just do it." Forget about how you feel, and just go for it. A few mini-hacks will help you along the way.

- Set your alarm. When you're scheduled to do something, make yourself excuse-proof.

- Make your bed as soon as you get up. That way, you'll be less tempted to climb back in. In a famous speech to the graduating class of the University of Texas at Austin in 2014, US Navy Admiral William H. McRaven said, "If you make your bed every morning you will have accomplished the first task of the day. It will give you a small sense of pride and it will encourage you to do another task and another and another. By the end of the day, that one task completed will have turned into many tasks completed. Making your bed will also reinforce the fact that little things in life matter. If you can't do the little things right, you will never do the big things right. **If you want to change the world, start off by making your bed.**"

- Hit the showers. Even if you're in autopilot mode, don't sit down at the kitchen table in a zombielike trance. Getting a shower right away gives you more motivation.

- Get dressed right away and *go.* No lingering. Don't give yourself time to stop and think. Sometimes you have to...say it with me now, "Just do it!"

- Plan your day and stick to it. Start small with accomplishing one thing and then add more to your to-do list each day. Post a letter, get the newspaper or milk from the store, walk the dog, take the trash out, buy some fresh flowers for your house, water the plants, go for a quick run at the park, get the car washed or fill it up with gas, etc. The important thing is setting a schedule and sticking to it, one task at a time, putting one leg in front of the other, taking step after step until you're back in the swing of things again.

Lifehack #40

Travel

Traveling is magic, which is why there are so many books where people talk about their life-changing journeys to foreign lands. Even on cramped economy flights, crowded buses and rickety trains, there's just something thrilling about packing up and visiting a destination you've never been to before. Well, guess what? Researchers have recently discovered how good travel is for your body and brain.

Experiencing new sights and sounds while traveling can set off the connections in your brain that are responsible for creativity. Traveling also prevents Alzheimer's disease and dementia among seniors. Additionally, people who travel report higher levels of general satisfaction in life, and are less likely to experience heart attacks.

This is because traveling has a wonderful way of decreasing levels of stress, and increasing levels of happiness in our minds and bodies. These benefits are not only enjoyed during the travel itself, but are experienced even after the travelers have gone home. However, the benefits of travel don't even begin when you set foot on a plane, train or automobile en route to your vacation spot. Even planning and preparing for your trip can already increase your overall wellbeing.

So what are you waiting for? If your job and schedule allow

you some time off, maybe it's time for your next trip. Oh, the places you'll go! I don't know about you, but for me, there's something about traveling, going on an adventure to somewhere I've never been, that excites me and lifts me up out of a funk like few other things can. I love everything about traveling, from planning to packing to getting on a train, plane, or in an automobile, and taking off for parts unknown. As the Dalai Lama wisely said, "Once a year, go someplace you've never been before."

Day Trip Ideas

- Visit an old Victorian Railway Station
- Go to a pub that's at least a couple of hundreds of years old
- Climb a Gothic Tower
- Go deer spotting in a park
- Try a historic river tour
- Take a walk around a Jacobean mansion
- Look for rare birds and wildlife
- Go somewhere funky like the Roald Dahl Museum
- See a medieval castle or prison

Weekend breaks. If you're going for an overnighter, there are nearby places all around that you can visit. I'm going to start off by writing about Scotland and Wales, although there are so many other places to go

My top 3 weekenders in Scotland:

1. The Isle of Skye—there's a reason why photographers love this place so much. The land and sea scapes, the wildlife, the Iron Age structures, the castles, the dinosaur footprints.... In other words, there's something for everyone. If you want to go somewhere dramatic, go for the Isle of Skye.

2. Edinburgh—whose history dates back to 900 BC, and where you can find a perfectly preserved Old Town. If you want to skip Old Town and New Town, there are many gardens, museums, and palaces to visit, as well as a zoo with a couple of giant pandas. For creatives, if you time your trip with the Fringe Festival or the Edinburgh Festival, there will be lots of sighs to gladden your soul.

3. The Highlands—aka the Outdoor Capital of the UK. Awaken your sense of adventure by climbing mountains, or go bird or rare animal watching, or oratory climbing Neptune's Staircase. Or you could always search for Nessie at Loch Ness.

My top 3 weekenders in Wales:

1. Snowdonia—Wales' biggest national park. Yes, you guessed it, I love the great outdoors passionately. Climb Mount Snowdon, the highest peak, or take the Mountain Railway, if you're feeling less adventurous. If you are a mountain biker,

this is a great place for you, with trails abounding everywhere. If heights are not your thing, go and visit the underground cave in Blaenau Ffestiniog, and check to their amazing trampoline.

2. Chepstow—with its walled town and lovely port, and a really old stone castle. Literature buffs will want to walk in the footsteps of William Wordsworth at Tintern Abbey or see the Hay-on-Wye arts and literary festival. Who can resist a place called the Wye Valley Area of Outstanding Natural Beauty?

3. Cardiff—If you love history, why not visit Cardiff Castle, built in 1106? The more modern minded among us can go shopping or do water sports, or catch a game of rugby or a concert at the Millennium Stadium. Dr Who fans are in for a special treat because of the Tardis Set at The Doctor Who Experience.

If you have a week or so, I have some suggestions that are off the beaten path, and are amazing places to visit.

1. Konjic, Bosnia and Herzegovina. Come for the bridges, beautiful churches and mosques, all near a lively river. Stay for the laid-back vibe. It's a wonderful place hardly anyone has heard of.

2. Carvoeiro, Portugal. It's a tiny fishing village in the southern part of the country, with plenty of charm of its own. Visit the

rock pools of Algar Seco and get some sun on the beach. It's guaranteed relaxation.

3. Pluzine, Montenegro. This is about as far off the beaten track as you can get. Pluzine is a small town right by a lake and surrounded by mountains. There are a lot of side trips to explore the canyons and rivers nearby, so you can get lost at will.

4. Bled, Slovenia. A stone's throw away from the capital, Ljubljana, Bled is a tiny island in the middle of the lake. All my best vacation spots center around water, can you tell? Visit the castle by the lake to taste a local specialty, Bled Cake. It's nature at its best whether in summer or winter.

5. Port de Soller, Spain. On the other, non-touristy side of Mallorca, this rustic place is the gateway to the path to Sa Mola Mountains. It's everything a quiet getaway spot should be, with a charming harbor and town well worth visiting.

If you plan to have a bit of a longer vacation, let me tell you about some awesome, budget-friendly destinations around the world.

1. Peru—If you've ever wanted to visit the ruins of Macchu Picchu, you'll find travel to Peru to be very affordable. You might also want to visit towns along the Andes highlands along the way. Meals and accommodations in Peru are not pricey at all.

2. Nepal—Come on, Mount Everest, right? And even if the country is still in recovery from a couple of severe earthquakes in 2015, you'll still find so much that is charming and unspoiled. Going to Nepal is like going to another world.

3. The Philippines—If you love the beach, the Philippines is perfect for you because some of the best beaches in the world are there. You may want to skip the capital, Manila, and go straight to the island of Palawan. Plus, the people are incredibly warm, welcoming, and helpful.

4. Egypt—Admit it, you've always wanted to see the pyramids, right? Traveling in Egypt will cost you less than $25 a day. It's one of the few places where it's easy and affordable to find vegetarian meals, too.

5. Malawi—This country is also known as "The Warm Heart of Africa" and is a true paradise for backpackers. You could easily get by on $10 a day or less.

Plus, it's a good starting point if you decide to visit Mozambique, Tanzania, and Zambia, which are all nearby.

Lifehack #41

Spend Some Time Alone

Sometimes, one of the best ways to get out of a funk is to decompress and get some time to yourself. It's good to take temporary timeouts from life's daily responsibilities, if they can wait for a bit or if someone can cover for you. Don't just disappear. Let your family or roommates know that you need a bit of a break and that you'll be back at the end of the day, ready for whatever tomorrow brings.

And then? Go to a museum and spend as much time as you like looking at the paintings that catch your eye. Have lunch by yourself in a nice cafe or restaurant. Go to the movies solo. Or go on a long solitary walk or hike where you have hours to yourself and nothing but the sounds of nature in your ear. If you need to cry, pray, chant, sing—do so. Do whatever it takes to restore your equanimity. I've needed days like these, when I didn't want to hear any other human voice for some hours at a time. I find silence and solitude to be greatly restorative, and I always come back feeling fresh and energized.

Here are two centering and calming things you can do during your alone time. How about de-stressing with a green smoothie and a DIY face mask?

A green smoothie is one of the quickest, easiest and most delicious ways to get much-needed nutrients into your system.

A few tips before you start:

- A good smoothie is always roughly 60 percent fruits and 40 percent greens.
- Always start with blending your greens with the liquid base, little by little to avoid chunky bits. Then add the fruit and blend again.
- Instead of adding ice, freeze the fruits instead. Bananas, berries, mangoes, grapes, pineapple can all be frozen in individual portions and used as needed. Come to think of it, you can also freeze your greens, too.
- Make your smoothies the night before to save you time in the morning. You can keep them in airtight containers in your refrigerator for up to 48 hours. Shake well before drinking.

Basic green smoothie recipe

Ingredients

2 cups spinach

2 cups water

1 cup mango, frozen

1 cup pineapple

2   bananas,   frozen

Instructions

Blend together spinach and water till all chunky pieces are gone. Add fruit and blend together until smooth. Enjoy!

Other green smoothie combinations:

- 2 c kale + 1 c water + 1 c cranberries + 2 oranges + 2 bananas (frozen)
- 1 c spinach + 1/4 c almond milk + 1/2 tsp vanilla + 1 banana (frozen) + 1 c avocado
- 1/2 c grapefruit juice + 1 c spinach or kale + 1 c apple + 1 c cucumber +3/4 c chopped celery + 1/3 c frozen mango +2 tsp mint leaves + 1 and 1/2 tsp coconut oil + 4 ice cubes

For DIY face masks—recreate a spa experience at home. Light a scented candle, put on some relaxing music, dim the lights. Come out rejuvenated and refreshed.

Some tips before you start:

- Test any mixture on a small spot behind your ear to check for allergies. Wait 24 hours. For how to do a patch test: https://www.reddit.com/r/SkincareAddiction/comments

- Apply the mask gently on your face without rubbing in.
- Masks should only be left on for 15 minutes, and then rinsed off.
- Only use masks once a week.

1. Basic Hydrating Mask

Combine 1/2 c oatmeal + 1/2 c water + 1/2 c milk + 1 tbsp honey in a small pan.

Cook over medium heat for 3-5 minutes, and let cool.

Apply to face when cool, and then rinse off after 15 minutes.

2. Breakout Prevention Mask

Combine 1/2 tsp lemon juice + 1/2 tsp baking soda + 1 tbsp honey and mix well.

Apply to face gently, do not scrub, and then rinse off after 15 minutes.

Be very careful with around your eye area as the lemon juice can sting.

3. Redness Treatment Mask

Mix 1 tsp Matcha green tea powder + 1/2 tsp coconut oil + 1/2 tsp water.

Apply to face, and rinse off after 15 minutes.

4. Tightening and Toning Mask

Mix one egg white with a fork or whisk, apply to face, and
    rinse off after 15 minutes.

5. Soothing Face Mask

Mix 1 tbsp. cooked pumpkin (or canned) +1 tsp topical
    Vitamin E oil + 1 tsp raw honey

Apply to face, and rinse off after 15 minutes.

Lifehack #42

Write Down A List Or Two

Lists can be a great coping mechanism when things feel rough or rocky. They can help you feel that you've regained control, especially when you feel that life is coming at you way too fast and you're having a hard time keeping up.

Writing lists can be a very calming activity, because they can help your brain feel organized. Lists can go from minutia such as the week's grocery shopping to be done, people you need to buy Christmas presents for, or can get as grand as an ultimate bucket list of places around the world you want to visit before you turn 50, or the top ten greatest movies of all time and why they're so outstanding.

Lists can be also introspective or reflective, like writing down and describing 5 things that make you happy, or the top three triggers that send you into an emotional tailspin. Lists can also be nostalgic, with you writing down the best birthday gifts you've ever received, or the best dogs your family had.

One of the nicer things about lists is the sense of accomplishment you get when you've accomplished certain items and you can cross them off, as you'd do on a to-do or a shopping list. Checking these off gives you a boost to your mood. Lists can also help you remember the good things in your life. My most favorite list is a gratitude list for the people and things I'm thankful for, and they inspire me to do something good in return for the good I've received.

Here is a list of some lists that you could write down on hectic or blue days. By the way, writing this list just made me feel a little better.

1. 10 Must-Dos Before You Reach Your Next Decade—places to go, things to learn, dishes to cook, etc.
2. 5 Life-Changing Books
3. 7 Must-Watch Documentaries
4. A Complete Guide to Throwing Your Next Dinner party, including
   a. The guest list
   b. The menu
   c. Shopping list
   d. Decor
   e. Playlist for the night
   f. Seating arrangements

5. The Top 8 Things I Love About Myself (physical attributes, strengths, skills)
6. The 9 Best People I Know
7. My Top 10 Favorite Things to Eat (appetizers, meals, desserts, fruit, chocolate, etc.)

8. 5 Things I'd Put In My Backpack in the Event of a Zombie Apocalypse

9. 3 Habits I'd Like to Develop Before the Year Ends

10. 4 Aliases I'd Like to Use At Least Once In My Life (write down the funny names you know you've always wanted to use)

Lifehack #43

Become an Artist

Art has been used for many years as a way for expressing your emotions through creative channels, and not just through talking. Therapists have used several forms of art for therapeutic purposes, including drawing, painting, sculpture, storytelling, dramatics, music and dance. The wonderful thing about expressing yourself though art is that you get to communicate your thoughts and feelings in new and creative ways—maybe even some feelings that have been hidden under the surface.

A lot of people talk about feeling like a burden is removed from their shoulders when they've expressed themselves through art, but don't think that art is only for the purpose of purging out negative feelings. On the contrary, creating artistic works actually results in many positive feelings as well.

Researchers have seen that expressing yourself creatively results in dopamine being released in your brain, which causes a surge of pleasurable feelings, decreasing feelings of depression and anxiety. But where should you start? I suggest a walk around a paper or crafts store, looking out for whatever catches your eye. If it's pencils and a sketchpad—go for it.

Or you could choose watercolors, or oil paints on canvas, or even modeling clay. Remember how satisfying it was to be in elementary school and to mold the clay in your hands, creating not just figures but entire landscapes or cityscapes? Alternatively, there's all sorts of crafts you can do—from quick DIY knickknacks or more elaborate art projects.

Making something artistic is one of my favorite depression hacks, and it really worked wonderfully for me. You see, I was so pleased and surprised to have created an adult coloring book a short while back. I found myself doodling one day and realized that it relaxed me and helped me combat depression.

Well, as time went on I kept doodling more and more, until I woke up to the fact that that I had enough material to fill a whole coloring book. Doing something I loved that was beautiful and creative helped me and made me happy, and I hope that it helps others as well. For those who are interested in it, it's called "Adult Coloring Book: Everyday in every way, I am getting better and better!: 40 Mandalas Stress reducing designs" and you can find it on Amazon.

Lifehack #44

Connect With Your Tribe

Did you know that having good relationships (and not necessarily romantic ones, either) is the biggest single indicator of the level of happiness, as well as longevity, in a person's life? When we're feeling down, staying connected with family and friends is key to our overall well-being. Humans are by nature social beings, and the loving support of our nearest and dearest is very important indeed.

However, how many of us have lost relationships because we were too sad/angry/out of it to stay closely connected to our friends and family, especially when we've needed them most. Maybe we've said or done hurtful things, or we were too absorbed in what we felt that we had very little time and space for the people we loved. If this is the case, don't worry, it's not too late to rebuild your tribe, one friend or family member at a time.

There is really only one way to reconnect with friends and family who may have fallen by the wayside—**reach out.** The good news is that there are a myriad of ways to reach out. Here's where you can get really creative. The most direct way is to call or text someone, but you can also send a friendly email or an old-fashioned card via snail mail. You can invite them to coffee or tea, a walk, a movie, or a meal. You can bring them a small thoughtful gift like a bunch of flowers, or something that you baked or cooked. What you want to do is let people know that you are thinking of them, that you care about them, and that you want to re-establish a meaningful connection with them.

If you know that your past actions have hurt others, you will need to make amends. I know I did. When my depression caused me to act very badly toward some beloved longtime friends, people who I went through a lot with, I needed to tell them how sorry I was that I hurt them. And it took a while before our friendship to go back to normal, but we all worked at it and are still working at it today.

Another thing you can do to expand the tribe you have is to make new friends. Social interactions are vital to your mental and emotional health, which is why one of the running threads in this book is to encourage all of us who have struggled with depression to get out there and be with people whose company we enjoy.

Even simple things like shopping at the local farmer's market, instead of buying everything you need online, can result in unexpected friendships as you find people with common interests or perspectives about life. When you do make new friends, don't feel obligated to talk about what you've gone through or how you feel. Keep it lighthearted, and if the conversation goes on to deeper topics and you feel safe about opening up, then do so. But there is no pressure to tell anyone everything—just have a great time together.

So call up a friend and see if they're free to meet up for coffee. Or else you can go on a walk or a run together, or see a movie. Another thing you could do is to help each other with chores or childcare, making everyday activities a little more fun with a friend by your side.

As the song goes, "People who need people, are the luckiest people in the world."

Lifehack #45

Take Pictures

This has never been easier, what with everyone's phone coming with a built-in camera that takes awesome photos. Surprisingly enough, taking pictures and self-portraits can be an effective way to beat the blues since it is another form of creative self-expression. Yes, photography is therapeutic and can make you feel a lot better.

How does photography help people overcome depression?

For one, when you take pictures you literally undergo a perspective change and see things from a different perspective. You also get involved with searching for beauty and meaning in the world, which lifts you out of your own headspace and causes you to focus on other things.

Thirdly, taking photographs gives you more control of how you frame the world around you. Additionally, photography can also be a valuable social experience when you share the pictures you took with others, and give and receive feedback from others about those photos.

There is even an online community of photographers for people who experience depression and anxiety called *The One Project*. Bryce Evans, one of the people behind *The One Project,* has a wonderful TEDx talk on photography and depression called *How Photography Saved My Life.*

Lifehack #46

Give Crystals A Try

Crystals have long been known to give off positive energy, but certain crystals help with depression by blocking and absorbing negative energy for you. Isn't that something?

These crystals end up protecting your energy so you can stay positive. Three crystals, in particular, are said to be particularly effective in fighting depression. You can carry them around with you, wear them around your neck or wrist, or keep them on your nightstand by your bed.

1. Lepidolite—this violet stone is said to be effective in absorbing obsessive thoughts. Because lepidolite has lithium, it can also act as a mood stabilizer, calming you down so you can make choices with confidence and a clear mind. It also helps you sleep well at night by balancing the energy you have in excess.

2. Smoky quartz—when you're feeling stressed and your nerves are frayed, and you've been getting less self-care time than usual, smoky quartz can help you as it's said to ground negative energy and calm you down. It's a mood lifter that lessens fearful feelings, giving you more tolerance and acceptance.

3. Tiger's Eye—long used as a charm to ward off ill wishes, this stone can be helpful when you're about to confront someone, or when you're in the presence of a negative person. Like the smoky quartz, it also grounds your energy and directs you to more positive thoughts and heightens self-love and self-worth, thus combating depression.

Lifehack #47

The Importance Of Affirmations

Affirmations are positive quotes or declarations that you read aloud to yourself to channel your thoughts into positive directions, and even create new ways of thinking. They run counter to negative self-talk that has the tendency to plague our minds and feelings. Many people who have used affirmations as part of their tools to fight depression have reported that these have been highly effective in their recovery. Since in the final part of this book I will be discussing affirmations at length, and will also give a number of examples, I will save a more detailed discussion on them for later.

I'd like to point out, however, that research has shown that the success of affirmations making a positive change to your mood depends on your commitment to practicing them consistently and regularly, i.e. setting aside time to do them every day. What's important, as well, is your confidence that the words you speak in an affirmation will take you in the direction that you want to go. In other words, choosing to believe in the affirmation is almost as important as the affirmation itself.

Lifehack #48

Start Working On A Project Again

Again, this is all about the power of creative expression and distracting yourself from your own thoughts and feelings through channeling your energies into something productive and positive. Projects are great for combating the blues because of the good feelings you get when you think and plan on creating and improving something, and then you anticipate how the project will turn out, and then end up enjoying the fruit of your labor.

I would say start by taking a walk around your house. Get out of bed and get moving! Projects are wonderful because they give you a reason to get up in the morning. Look around and see what you can tackle. Do you want to renovate a certain room by repainting the walls with a fresh color? Or do you want to go through every nook and cranny of your kitchen (including your refrigerator), and throw out anything you haven't used in at least a year? Do you want to sew new curtains for your living room, or build new pieces of furniture to replace items that have been around since your grandparents' time?

Maybe a self-improvement project is more up your alley. You could immerse yourself in learning a new language, or upgrading your cooking, baking, or carpentry skills. These self-improvement lessons won't break your bank account either.

There are many free resources on the internet that are extremely helpful. Don't forget to set goals for yourself—specific things like "in three months I'll be 20 percent fluent in Mandarin" or "in two weeks I'll have mastered cooking a Thai entree, main dish, and desert."

If you're interested, here are some free language apps that also track your progress:

- Duolingo—https://www.duolingo.com
- Busuu—https://www.busuu.com/en/mobile
- Rosetta Stone—https://www.rosettastone.com/lp/mobile-apps/

Lifehack #49

Do *Something* You're Good At

If you make killer brownies that everyone loves, do it today. If you've got an amazing green thumb, work it. Grow some plants like the boss you are. If you used to be the champion bowler in your neighborhood, take it up again. If knitting or crochet is your specialty, start making Christmas gifts for the people you care about. Get the picture?

Okay, so why is this so important? We who experience depression often have a debilitating self-critical voice in our heads that loves to tell us about our failures over and over again, ad infinitum, ad nauseam. We pretty much learn to live with those voices that tell us about every area where we don't do well.

Well, we need the opposite when we're feeling the blues.

We need praise. Do you remember how it felt when you were a child and your parents and teachers praised your abilities in math or art, or when you recited a poem particularly well? That felt pretty great, didn't it? So back to doing things you're good at. When you do things well, you receive positive feedback, grateful and admiring words that praise you for a job well done, that can do wonders for drowning out the other voices. These words help you believe in yourself again, and feel good about yourself again.

So do what you're good at and do it over and over again!

Lifehack #50

Listen To A Podcast

There has never been a time when so many interesting, funny, informative, and fascinating listening materials have been available to us as now. Instead of listening to the news about what a certain interesting world leader Tweeted this morning or about that other interesting head of state threatening to send bombs halfway around the world—stuff that can just add to your sadness, confusion, or anger—why not listen to a really great podcast that will put a smile on your face or a spring in your step?

Podcasts have changed my life. Instead of only listening to the music when I go for a walk or a run, I listen to the week's episode of *Dear Sugar* or *Modern Love* from *The New York Times*. I also love hearing preaching podcasts when I can't get to church, and when I drive or while commuting or traveling, my favorite podcasts keep me company.

Podcasts now cover any and every area of interest, and you can tailor-fit your listening list for however you're feeling at any given time. Whether you feel like hearing more about the latest tech developments, politics, science, true crime, history, food, entertainment, and just life in general, you'll find something that will satisfy you. Best of all is that so many of these are free. There's a podcast for everyone, no matter how quirky or eccentric your tastes are.

Here's a list of some really good podcasts that came out in the past couple of years.

- Savage Lovecast—Dan Savage's weekly advice on sex and relationships.
- The Home Front: Life in America During World War II—narrated by Martin Sheen, aka the best President the US (n)ever had.
- Lore—by Aaron Mahnke, which is about real life spooky stories. They're fairly short and not so scary that they'll give you nightmares, and often come with a mini history lesson.
- Song Exploder—where musicians tell the story of how their songs were written.
- Last but not least, The Hilarious World of Depression—where host John Moe talks to comedians and other funny people who have battled with clinical depression, often using comedy. This podcast is a lifesaver, and I could not love it more. You'll find it on iTunes.

Lifehack #51

Remember You Are Not Alone...

A whole lot of famous people in history, and even some celebrities today, have also battled with depression. If it were a club and you looked around, you'd realize that some well-known people have felt the same way you do. So the next time you feel depressed, do a little bit of research on one of the following people. How they overcame depression and went on to do amazing things in their lives can be a source of courage and inspiration for you.

Hans Christian Andersen * Charles Baudelaire * Kristen Bell * Ingmar Bergman * Halle Berry * Beyoncé * David Bohm * Ludwig Boltzmann * Kjell Magne Bondevik * Jon Bon Jovi * Marlon Brando * Wayne Brady * Zach Braff * Charles Bukowski * Barbara Bush * Truman Capote * Jim Carrey * Mary Chapin Carpenter * Johnny Carson * Helena Bonham Carter * Johnny Cash * Ray Charles * Chevy Chase *Agatha Christie * Winston Churchill * Eric Clapton * Leonard Cohen * Joseph Conrad * Catherine Cookson * Calvin Coolidge * Jeb Corliss * Courteney Cox * Sheryl Crow * Louis C.K. * Ellen DeGeneres * Cara Delevingne * Diana, Princess of Wales * Charles Dickens * Emily Dickinson * Fyodor Dostoyevsky * Bob Dylan, American * Harlan Ellison* Chris Evans * Chris Farley * William Faulkner * Gabriel Fauré * Craig Ferguson * F. Scott Fitzgerald * Michel Foucault * Stephen Fry * Peter

Gabriel *Gaston Gaudio * Donald Glover * Johann Wolfgang von Goethe * Joseph Gordon-Levitt * Tipper Gore * Francisco de Goya *Kelsey Grammer * Graham Greene * Jon Hamm * Friedrich August Hayek * Geoffrey Hill * Hulk Hogan * Sir Anthony Hopkins * Natalie Imbruglia * Janet Jackson * William James * Billy Joel * Dwayne Johnson * Samuel Johnson * Angelina Jolie * Kevan Jones * Ashley Judd * Franz Kafka * Hamid Karzai * John Keats * Jack Kerouac * Marian Keyes * Alicia Keys * Søren Kierkegaard * Martin Luther King, Jr. * Stephen King * Ernst Ludwig Kirchner * Anne Kirkbride * John Kirwan * Shane Koyczan * Akira Kurosawa * Lady Gaga * Kendrick Lamar * Hugh Laurie * Lecrae *John Lennon * Neil Lennon

Plus...

David Letterman * Lee Joon-gi * Meriwether Lewis * Richard Lewis * Abraham Lincoln * Mary Todd Lincoln * Heather Locklear * Oscar Lopez * Demi Lovato * Howie Mandel * Shirley Manson * John Marsden * Henri Matisse *Guy de Maupassant * Brian May * Vladimir Mayakovsky* Ewan McGregor * Herman Melville * Charlotte Mew * Michelangelo * John Stuart Mill * Spike Milligan * Kylie Minogue * Joan Miró *Joni Mitchell * Moby *Alanis Morissette * Morrissey * Wolfgang Amadeus Mozart * Bill Murray *

Isaac Newton * Friedrich Nietzsche * Trevor Noah * Graeme Obree * Conan O'Brien * Eugene O'Neill * Robert Oppenheimer * Marie Osmond * Dolly Parton * Deepika Padukone * János Pilinszky * Brad Pitt * Edgar Allan Poe *Jackson Pollock * Richard Pryor * Sergei Rachmaninoff * Charlotte Rampling * Ayn Rand *Anne Rice * R Rainer Maria Rilke * John D. Rockefeller * Richard Rodgers * Mark Rothko * Ronda Rousey *J. K. Rowling * Bertrand Russell *

And...

Antoine de Saint-Exupéry* Matthew Santoro * Siegfried Sassoon * Charles M. Schulz * Frank Sinatra * Brooke Shields * Sarah Silverman * Rick Springfield * Bruce Springsteen * Charles Spurgeon * Nicolas de Staël * Gwen Stefani * Rod Steiger * Sting * August Strindberg * William Styron * Amy Tan * Catherine Tate * Channing Tatum * James Taylor * Pyotr Ilyich Tchaikovsky * Emma Thompson * Hunter S. Thompson * Uma Thurman * T.I. * The Notorious B.I.G. * Leo Tolstoy * Lars von Trier * Mark Twain * Mike Tyson * Eddie Vedder * Kurt Vonnegut * Mike Wallace * Kerry Washington * Evelyn Waugh * Otto Weininger *Florence Welch * Jonathon

Welch * Kanye   West * Wil   Wheaton * Walt
Whitman * Kevin Whitrick * Robbie Williams * Robin
Williams * Steven Williams * Tennessee Williams *
William Carlos Williams *Brian Wilson * Owen
Wilson *Gregory Wilton * Dean Windass * Oprah
Winfrey * Ludwig   Wittgenstein * Lewis
Wolpert * Virginia Woolf * Michael Yardy * Thom
Yorke

When I look at those names I can't help but remember that
there are millions of people around the world who are
experiencing depression every single day. I'm not alone, and
neither are you. The good news is that depression isn't the
end of your journey, but simply a part of it. Your story is yours
to write.

I hope you've made your own list of effective lifehacks that
make depression more bearable and give you the push you
need. Don't just choose one, but I do encourage you to try as
many as you can so that you have several in your arsenal that
you can pull out and use any time. Knowing what helps us feel
better makes the road we walk on a little bit easier.

Lifehack #52

Mantras

I've put together lists of some powerful mantras that you can try for yourself on days when you need an extra mental and emotional lift to get you through life's demands. As I've said earlier, words not only have power, they **are** power. What you say charts the path ahead for yourself. And if you are battling depression, it's all too easy for the seemingly ever-present negative thoughts to get you to go down an equally negative path. You see, thoughts are also words—spoken only in your mind—but they also have the power to affect you greatly. Sad, pessimistic, fearful, angry, or any other negative thought can send you down a negative path.

One wonderful way to fight that is through mantras and affirmations. Now, why don't we make the distinction between the two before we go any further? First of all, mantras have been used for many centuries now. They are sacred syllables or poems, originally in Sanskrit, and have been used along with the practice of meditation. Mantras are an important part of Hindu traditions, and are practiced in Buddhism and other religions in India as well. The word mantra itself comes from "man," which means to think, and "tra," meaning to set free. Hence, *mantras* are used to set one's mind free.

In the traditional sense, mantras have two parts—significance and sound, or the meaning of the actual words chanted, as well as the vibrations that the sounds produce.

The simplest mantra is the word *Om*—which is believed to be the primary vibration of the universe. It is the most potent and fundamental mantra, and all Vedic prayers incorporate this sound. Perhaps it would be easy to explain "Om" this way: chanting "Om" focuses on the One truth. When reciting their mantras, many people use Hindu bead necklaces called *malas,* which have 108 beads in all, in order to make sure that they reach 108 repetitions. Other religions, including Judaism, Islam, and Christianity, have also used repetitive chanting in their prayers.

Affirmations, on the other hand, are statements used to train our thought processes to move toward positive results. In the 1970's, neuroscientists used their understanding of language and therapy and began to use positive affirmations to help patients change the way they perceived life. Affirmations are usually sentences that state a desired outcome as though one already possessed it.

Mantras and affirmations have worked best in those who put their belief behind the words they say. It important that in choosing a mantra or an affirmation, you find words that resonate deeply with you, so that you can put your full confidence in repeating them.

Mantras and affirmations have shown to be effective in

- Decreasing levels of anxiety and stress
- Helping improve relationships
- Boosting self-confidence
- Clearing the mind from worry and negativity

12 Modern Mantras That You Can Use:

1. **"There is nothing that can hurt me here."** Living with depression and anxiety can sometimes make you feel like you're in fight or flight mode all the time. You feel afraid of practically anything and everything. Repeating, "There is nothing that can hurt me here," to yourself over and over while you practice deep breathing and you picture yourself safe and sound can produce a calming effect that can slow your heart rate down and even lower your blood pressure. What you're doing in reciting this mantra is telling your brain that you are not in danger, that the scary things that pop up in your imagination are not real, and that you are free to live life. You're free to do everything that you need to do throughout the day, and no harm will come to you.

2. **"If I can make it through the next ten seconds, I can make it through anything."** Again, when the anxious voices in your head are screaming loudly and you feel like you hear sirens and alarm bells everywhere, it's not very pleasant at all. This is one way to break up that panicky feeling into manageable, bite-sized pieces. Breathe deeply and repeat the sentence again and again until the panic passes. This mantra is great for reassuring yourself that everything will work out, that you just need to wait out some frenzied feelings for a little while. But you will be fine when it's done. A shorter, more concise version of this is, **"This too shall pass."** It's a good reminder that feelings, no matter how intense, are temporary.

3. **"I trust the process, because new beginnings arise from hard times."** This is a good mantra of acceptance, an adaptation of sorts of Reinhold Niebhur's well-known Serenity Prayer ("God grant me the serenity to accept the things I cannot change; courage to change the things I can; and wisdom to know the difference," which is also a pretty great mantra to adapt as well.) This mantra is powerful in dispelling fears in uncertain situations, or when you feel impatient because your progress or growth in certain areas seems slow. It is also a good mantra for changing your mindset to embrace and welcome new situations that are

outside your comfort zone, as opposed to facing these with dread or fear.

4. **"Breathing in, I know that I am breathing in. Breathing out, I know that I am breathing out."** This is a mantra for mindful breathing from Thich Nhat Hanh, a Vietnamese Zen Buddhist monk who wrote a book called <u>**You Are Here**</u>. Hanh explains that it is mindful breathing that connects our minds and bodies, and when we focus on our breathing, we are able to achieve calmness and relaxation more quickly. Thus, in situations where you feel like panicking, this is a good mantra to repeat until you feel peaceful and calm again.

Hanh suggests other mantras along the same lines, including:

For the times when you need refreshing. **"Breathing in, I see myself as a flower. Breathing out, I feel fresh."**

For the times when you need stability. **"Breathing in, I see myself as a mountain. Breathing out, I feel solid."**

For the times you need stillness. **"Breathing in, I see myself as still as water. Breathing out, I reflect things as they are."**

For the times you need freedom. **"Breathing in, I see myself as space. Breathing out, I feel free."**

Why not try one of these on and see what works best for you?

5. **"Someday this will all make sense."** This is a wonderful mantra to repeat to yourself when you feel confused or puzzled at the things that have happened to you and around you, and you do not and indeed cannot understand why they happened. Breathe in and breathe out slowly with this mantra, letting go of every lingering question, especially the ones that begin with "Why?" This mantra will help you accept that there are certain things we just won't understand now, but they'll get clearer in the weeks, months, or years to come. With this mantra you accept your own finite perception as a human being, but you trust that one day, you will know all things. Christians have a version for this—"We'll understand it better by and by."

6. **"My healing and wholeness are on the way."** With this mantra, you are declaring to the universe that not only will you feel better, you will get better. When repeating this mantra, emphasize different words each time—for example, say it the first time putting an emphasis on the first

word. **"MY healing and wholeness are on the way."**

On the second time, emphasize the second word. **"My HEALING and wholeness are on the way."** On the third time, emphasize the third word. **"My healing AND wholeness are on the way."** On the fourth time, emphasize the fourth word. **"My healing and WHOLENESS are on the way."** You get the picture, right? This way, you are reaching out for every good promise and potential that is in that mantra, and taking it for yourself. No matter how you bad you feel when you got up that morning, or how many setbacks you may have suffered, you are taking a stand for your own healing and wholeness.

7. **"I forgive myself and let go of my past. Even if my past was just a little while ago."** As I've said before, living with depression at times feels like living with a person inside your head whose favorite pastime is to remind you of all the wrong things you've ever done. At night, just before you go to sleep, this voice just loves to rehearse the screw-ups you did that day, trying to prevent you from getting good rest, and sometimes succeeding. So nighttime is a good time for this mantra. For as many times as that accusing voice comes to you, counter each time by repeating these two sentences. Remember, the fighter that stays in the battle longest wins, and so you'll need to stick it out,

breathing deeply, until the accuser is gone and you're able to sleep. A shorter version of this is "I let it go," or simply, "I let go."

8. **"A journey of a thousand miles begins with a single step."** With this mantra, Chinese philosopher Lao Tzu's famous words, you acknowledge that you still have a way to go, but you have gathered the courage to take the first step. You are taking a proactive stance toward your healing and wholeness. You may still feel fear and uncertainty, but you refuse to allow them to be stumbling blocks on your triumphant journey. With this mantra you know that after you take the first step, all you need to do is take the next one. And then the next. And then the next. You know that step after step will actually create a rhythm, a pace that becomes easier and easier the farther along you get. You strengthen your resolve and determination with every step you take until you reach the end of your journey.

Let me also include some traditional mantras in Sanskrit.

9. **"Om Namah Shivaya."** This is a traditional Sanskrit mantra that popular author Elizabeth Gilbert calls the "Amazing Grace of Sanskrit" in her bestselling book, *Eat, Pray, Love*. The literal translation of the chant is, "I bow to Shiva, the

supreme deity of transformation, who represents the truest, highest self." Gilbert, however, translates it as "I honor the divinity within myself."

Depression can take a terrible toll on our sense of worth, and this mantra is especially helpful for those who realize that they need their self-esteem and confidence to be built up. It also causes us to regard ourselves as more than just earthly beings, and when we realize that we are made up of celestial energy, we begin to be kinder and more respectful of ourselves. Shiva, as destroyer, is a symbol for the inner being that stays alive and whole even after everything else is destroyed, which gives us a clue to the power of this mantra.

10. **"Om Sarvesham Svastir Bhavatu."** This is known as the universal peace prayer.

"Sarveśām Svastir Bhavatu

Sarveśām Shāntir Bhavatu

Sarveśām Pūrnam Bhavatu

Sarveśām Maṇgalam Bhavatu"

Which translates as,

"May there be happiness in all

May there be peace in all

May there be completeness in all

May there be success in all."

This is a very good mantra when you're faced with a lot of bad news about the different conflicts in the world, and you feel all kinds of turmoil and negativity. It restores calmness, peace, and positivity in otherwise dark times. "Om Sarvesham Svastir Bhavatu," the universal peace prayer, also releases blessings into the world through you. As you strive to regain peace and calm for your own soul, you are also speaking it to every other being on the planet, which is a pretty powerful thing. Let your mind and body be conduit for positivity and good through mantras such as these.

Legendary musician Tina Turner gathered some children and together, they have an amazing recitation of this mantra and you can find it on YouTube.

11. The Shanti Mantras

Here is one example of the Shanti Mantras

"O ṃsaha nāv avatu

saha nau bhunaktu

saha vīrya ṃkaravāvahai

tejasvi nāv adhītam astu

mā vidviṣāvahai

Om śānti ḥśānti ḥśāntiḥ"

Which translates as:

May God protect us together; may God nourish us together;
May we work together with great energy,
May our endeavors be vigorous and effective;
May we not mutually dispute (or may we not hate any).
Let there be peace in me!
Let there be peace in my environment!
Let there be peace in the forces that act on me.

This is a good mantra for starting the day on a very positive note, or when you are thinking of the people around you and want have relationships that are positive and healthy. Reciting this brings you into a greater state of calmness and clarity, as well as removes all the physical, internal and outside obstacles that may be in your way. The word "Shanti" means peace, and this mantra always ends with saying "Shanti" three times in succession.

You can hear an example of the Shanti Mantra being recited on YouTube.

12. *"Lokah Samastah Sukhino Bhavantu."* Similar to the universal peace prayer, the Lokah Samastah Sukhino Bhavantu serves the dual purpose of bringing you to a place of peace and clarity, as well as allowing you to serve as a channel of blessing to the universe. It is translated as, "May all beings everywhere be happy and free, and may the thoughts, words, and actions of my own life contribute in some way to that happiness and to that freedom for all."

Through this mantra, one is able to move beyond his or her own concerns and participates in the concerns of all of humanity. Since depression has a way of making our lives very small and narrow, mantras such as these allow us to broaden and expand in our perspectives and consciousness. In short, when we repeat the *Lokah Samastah Sukhino Bhavantu,* we move from the personal to the global, as we are reminded that we are part of a much bigger whole, and more than that, we can make a positive contribution to everyone else in the world. The *Lokah Samastah Sukhino Bhavantu* has long been used in meditation to increase compassion and empathy for others, as well as bring about deep peace and calm. Perhaps closest in meaning to this mantra are the words of St Francis of Assisi—"Make me an instrument of thy peace." This mantra is powerful in helping foster cooperation and harmony among us all.

Printed in Great Britain
by Amazon